REVEALED

Reptilian Bloodlines

Or

Gog & Magog?

REVEALED

Reptilian Bloodlines

Or

Gog & Magog?

....

Mustapha M Jalloh

Dedication

This book is dedicated to God

CONTENTS

	Page
1. Mankind and Religion	10
2. The God, Creation: Angels/Jinns and Men	21
3. Yeshua (Jesus) and Muhammad	31
4. Anti-Christ: Age of the Anti-Christ	43
5. Gog & Magog and Cyrus 'the great'	51
6. Pelasgus: The Pelasgians; Danaids, Dorians & Archaeans; Arcadians	63
7. Pandora: Rhesus factor [Avatars]	72
8. Dionysian Mysteries [Attis & Cybele]	83
9. Greco-Roman Paganism: Titans & Olympians [Ceres-Liber-Libera]	96
10. Myths: Jason and the Argonauts	106
11. The Loa (Divination)	112
12. The Ascended Masters	117
13. Paganism & Catholicism	120
14. Arius: First Council of Nicaea	135
15. Original Incarnation: Philosopher's Stone & Rosicrucianism	145
16. Nature of the Incarnates	160
17. Ancient Egypt, Cleopatra and the Egyptian Tragedy	167
18. Arthur, Britannia and Marianne	174
19. My Story	188

20. Anti-Christ and the Jews	200
21. Renaissance, Science & Deception	208
22. Friedrich 'the great', Hitler	219
23. Age of Oppression	226
24. Conspiracies & Terrorism	235
25. Portrayals in society and popular culture	244
26. The Representative	255
27. Retaking our world	261

Mankind and Religion

Most men in their late teens or early twenties in this age reach the point of life when they first begin to question their existence and purpose.

This is often followed by an embrace of a belief in God. Maintaining such a belief (a belief in God) is commonly difficult because of the activities and covert, subtle agencies which cleverly and quite convincingly dissuade us from such trends.

For those of us fortunate enough, we learn about God and the Creation Story shared in the Torah, Bible and Qur'an.

The stories we are taught about God during this childhood period, clearly fills us with love for the Creator and gives us restful hope and care for the promised meeting (Day of Resurrection). Traditionally, we are told about the enemy (Satan) and adjured to be cautious, especially regarding him.

At present, we barely hold on to this advice – with the enemy now even being regarded as one who was wronged. Therefore, there is need to go back to the First Sin (Satan's Sin); Satan's refusal to do what God commanded – and gradually expose the reason for why the world is at present embracing Satan.

I shall narrate the version in Islam but also mention and give reasons for not using the Christian/Jewish version.

Adam, as in the Bible, was given life by an essence from God. God, after fashioning Adam out of clay, breathed of his Spirit into Adam, and by this he was brought to life.

This is not so with the other creatures who God commanded to prostrate to Adam.

Satan, out of haughtiness, was the only one who refused to prostrate to Adam, and so, disobeyed God. More so, he did not repent or ask God for forgiveness. Satan rejected being subordinate to Adam.

For him, Adam was not superior to him. He cited Adam's creation from clay and his creation from fire in explaining his refusal. This was the First Sin.

Satan is a Jinn (a type of Angel). One major distinguishing feature of Jinns from the rest of Angels is that they procreate (they sexually reproduce). They are of male and female sexes. Their wings as well are different to that of other angels.

This first sin of course preceded that of Adam's. Thus, you may see one possible flaw with the other account which sees Adam's sin as the original Sin.

As a result of Satan's disobedience (his given name in the Qur'an is "Iblis") and his turning away and rejection of faith in God, he drew God's promise of a punishment from Him.

God, though, granted respite to him until the Last Hour, in response to a request for this.

Iblis vowed to subdue Men (perhaps as a way to prove that Adam was not superior to him).

When Adam disobeyed God by doing what he was told not to do – after his wife who Satan had whispered to convinced him to sin, he repented. He sought God's forgiveness unlike Satan.

It is important to always note what God told Adam.

He said: Go. I will send you guidance. Whoever follows this guidance will be saved.

This guidance has come to us in the form of Books through prophets appointed to work to remind us of who we are, how we got to this point and what awaits us.

Making use of these messages is the most crucial part of our lives – especially now that we are in dire straits, with wars, tyranny, poverty, economic hardship, bullying and severe disunity.

The Qur'an tells us that Satan is our enemy. Therefore, we should take him also as an enemy.

Man is kind and is not fully aware of his world. As such, you may even want to forgive Satan. The nature of his enmity for us however, makes this completely unviable.

You have been offered a higher place to the Jinn. That which was breathed into you comes with its rights and place in life, so long as you are in turn obedient and fulfilling of your duties and as well careful in falling victim to Satan, you will not lose this position. Those who fall prey to, follow and associate themselves or others as equals with God will be punished and brought low. Associating and setting up partners with God or worshipping Satan is the sin which takes man to Hell.

Religion or better put, the 'right lifestyle' is the instrument to aid us live life successfully and least of toil in every sphere of life.

Since our creation, Iblis and those who support him have constantly plotted for us to fail and suffer – pre-earth, here on earth and post-earth. He and his followers see us but we do not see them.

The enemy has employed both short and long-term plans.

Using the respite which he was given, the enemy has undertaken and carried out a sophisticated system of deceit – deceiving us about ourselves and about God. It is only by faith and hope in God and with the help of true knowledge revealed, that his plans and schemes are exposed to us. This is why religion has come under subtle attacks, which takes many forms and ideas, in recent times. By this, they have been able to deceive many about God, with most people poorly informed and thus, ill-prepared to withstand the enemy's plots.

Islam for instance has suffered particular demonization from outside and within since the information and tools available to aid men through this age are contained in its revelations. I wish therefore in part, to expose to you some of these revelations that are now under both internal sabotage and external attacks, in light of its enlightening qualities.

'The God' or Allah

Allah is Arabic which means [The God]. Men believe in Angels – besides who are other creatures, like the animals on earth.

If there were only one man, he could be accurately called 'The Man'. But there are many Men. This is the same also with the Angels. If there were only one Angel, that angel may as well be accurately called 'The Angel'. But no angel enjoys this designation because there are many Angels.

There is one who is God. And only He is God. He is neither man nor angel etc. He is God.

Being God and being totally unique with no other being who shares His characteristics, He is 'The God'.

You may call Him, The Creator, The Sustainer, The Originator etc. and many others of His names.

In Arabic, 'The God' is Allah (Al [The] and i-lah [God]). As per the language, the 'i' is omitted in the contraction. Together, Allah reads as "The God". I doubt if this needs further explanation.

Clearly, the name shows his oneness, separateness and uniqueness. The saying: 'La ilaha illa llah' emphasizes and clarifies this. It means: "There is no god but The God".

The English name "God" (with capital) is good to use. Therefore I have opted to use it in this treatise in order to aid our unity.

The French word "Dieu" should not be used for God as it stems from "Zeus" (pagan Greek deity).

This brings me to Monotheism, and how this is the most important, most fundamental point of the Abrahimic Faiths.

Opposed to or different from this was the belief in two or more gods. Basically, the prophets, from the time of Noah, up until the Christian period held a strict and pure faith in one God and opposed and fought against those who would preach or seek to introduce a belief in more than one God. Together with a righteous lifestyle, nothing else was preached. This distinct, unique mark was its perennial identity throughout history.

Unlike what most of us have come to believe, Monotheism was practiced by not just the Israelites but as well, non-

Israelite nations like the Egyptians, who called 'The God', 'Amun'.

It was the attempt to change from this Monotheism at one time that caused the instability and subsequent demise of the Pharaoh, Akhenaten, who persecuted the Israelites. Other examples of Monotheistic religions included 'Zoroastrianism', which of course, suffered corruption.

Confucius of Ancient China was another of those regarded as a Monotheist.

Abraham's pure Monotheism is one of the hallmarks of belief in the one God and a struggle in this cause.

Moses' Ten Commandments which basically start by underlining the need for a belief in one God was the continuation of this propagation.

Based on the revelatory resources available to us, the worship, practice and history of Monotheism, no room or incontrovertible evidence exists for accommodating a belief in more than one God.

The enemy, in his quest to deceive Man has propagated many falsities like telling men they are evolved apes. With the help of Science and technology, he has also been successful in convincing many that they are beings who have evolved over time into the capable and highly sophisticated beings they now are – able possibly to even create life (i.e. beyond the present scientific and technological advances).

As such, most of the educated proudly lean toward or profess a belief in Atheism. Religion appears backward, and the norm is to see it as a means by which politicians and clerics aim to control or manipulate people.

Alongside this is the constant noise and clamor about 'freedom'. This freedom, to the keen observer, is not only political and social freedom.

I do not want to be misinterpreted for someone who does not accept or believe in the basic right of every individual to be free – so long as that freedom does not encroach on the rights of another or threaten the progress and stability of each individual polity.

Yet, based on the manner, tone and intensity of the calls and discourse, I am inclined to think that the freedom philosophy and agitation has deeper roots - with leanings along the story of Adam and Iblis (his refusal to accept his place). Beyond this, there is no such thing as unlimited freedom, and this further exposes the flaws of their aims. This work shall in its course expose more on this premise.

Israelites & Non-Israelites

The assumption that prophets were only sent to the Israelites is a false assumption and one that caused much havoc, like disunity.

If this was the case, some would rightly then say that others were left without any guidance, and that their nations did not benefit among the blessed Elect of God. Hence, Muhammad and other men from different nations were sent and chosen among their people to propagate good guidance.

In any attempt to discuss religion, a consistent challenge is proving God truly exists. The answer to that question I believe can be found within every man who is true to himself, and who carefully investigates himself.

The question whether it ends when you die: That you are to eat, sleep, procreate, live up to 80 or so years and then become nothing – after all the dreams, imagination, and wishes. In short, an ultimate tragedy in a life stuffed with pleasures and progress.

Or this earth, full of sustenance, beauty and design, that fits us well; existing within the restful darkness of the night and the exuberant livelihood of the day – both so enjoyable, in spite of the marked contrast of both – the night fitting well with the physical clock of the body.

Or we may apply current scientific knowledge of Space to it: This Earth that has existed for millions of years, with not once an accident involving a giant body (large asteroid, comet or some massive matter), able to cause irrecoverable damage ever colliding with the earth. These may convince us of God, Creator and Sustainer.

Per chance, this coupled with the arduous efforts of men who strove so hard to tell us; stressing the existence of a Creator who is different from all and infinitely great in might.

Add to this, men who have sighted the extraordinary, like angels or have experienced the activities of Jinns. This book shall in its course, hopefully, elucidate on this.

Our history and current events and culture now further present us with quite concrete evidences, unraveling those things that could only be believed with faith – therefore confirming the truth of the Prophets.

As for the truth and authenticity of Muhammad's prophet hood, hardly a mind would dispute this today, in light of how much he has been proved right and his prophecies regarding the Anti-Christ.

Earlier I stated that I would use the Islamic story of Satan's disobedience and that I would explain why I have not used the other account.

These accounts tell little about Satan's rejection of his place under Adam, and go further to allude and insinuate that there was a great fight in heaven. This would be totally untrue since a creature or creatures would find it impossible to orchestrate any such sacrilege in per se God's presence.

Secondly, God is an infallible God of great, infinite might. I am sure that His mere word would be enough to deal with such sacrilege.

Personally, I consider this an attempt to undermine our impression of God and His infinite majesty. In reverse, it seems to inflate our opinions of Satan and whatever stature he is seen to possess.

Better so, the story in the Qur'an which mentions Satan as the only one who refused to accept God's command further confirms the overwhelming acceptance of God's decision.

The other narrations appear to portray Satan as some great angel who wields enormous power. This notion, hence, gives credence, bolstering current attempts by these rebels to convince the world of some prospective alternative to God.

The God, Creation: Angels/Jinns and Men

Once more, 'The God', is the name for "the One". This entity is God, and there are no two entities like Him or even close. He is in a category of His own that is unshared. This name is definite, and describes clearly His position.

Knowing the One who is 'The God' requires a look at some revealed attributes.

'The God' is the Originator of the heavens and the earth and what is between them. His Throne is uncreated and is established above, over the seven Heavens and the earth.

When there was nothing else or total void, there was God. It is He who made, and with time added to what He created. The idea that the Creator is God because of His creative attribute is incomplete and erroneous. About four billion years ago, He created the Angels. The Jinns were created much later – probably one million years ago.

It is useful to discuss the almost exclusive name used for God in Islam, "Allah".

Muslims have failed to adequately enlighten non-Muslims about the name and their almost exclusive use of the name when even communicating in English. This has made some conceive of the name as different from the English, God, or perhaps even referring to another deity and not the God of Abraham, Moses and the Biblical prophets. This failure of

Muslims to adequately correct misconceptions about the name, whilst using it exclusively to refer to God is while astonishing, perhaps even deliberate. I should like to note however, that some names for God are inappropriate. One such name is "Dieu" (French), which stems from the Greek, Zeus (pagan god).

Angels

"All praise is due to God, Originator of the Heavens and the earth, (who) made the Angels messengers having wings, two or three or four. He increases in creation what He wills. Certainly, God has power over all things." [Qur'an 35:1]

Angels are of different nations and grades. The verse mentions the Angels as having two, three or four wings; indicating different grades. It is by these grades that they occupy the heavens; from the first to the seventh heaven.

The Jinns are a nation of Angels that are well marked in difference; sharing characteristics like sex and sexually reproducing. They have wings resembling those we see on Butterflies, and on fairies; which are not shared by the rest of Angels, and fly at a much slower pace.

Based on a narration of Muhammad, I would put the number of Angels aside Jinns at twenty-one trillion and Jinns, not exceeding two billion.

Satan portrayed with wings (Butterfly-like) like I noted

The Heavens

God is established on the Throne. Beneath it are the Seven Heavens, in layers; one above the other. The first of these is the one nearest to us, neighboring the stars.

Consider the universe as billions of light years in expanse. The seven heavens exist; stretching over the expanse of the universe. These seven heavens are the home of the Angels, and at one time the abode of the Jinns. It is beneath the Throne of God where no angels reside.

The fraudulent great fight in Heaven would have taken place here between twenty-one trillion angels and some two billion Jinns at most, who are far inferior in abilities. Angels (not Jinns) were made from light and are neither male nor female in sex.

The Jinns

The Jinns were made from smoke-free fire and like all Creation are not exempt from serving God. At some point they were sent together with Adam and Eve to inhabit earth. We share the earth but our worlds do not meet.

There is a place in Greek mythology called Elysium that is the likely home of Jinns. Plutarch mentions Elysium in his "Life of Sertorius". It would exist over an area we cannot grasp with our eyes or come into physical contact with.

"They enjoy moderate rains at long intervals, and winds which for the most part are soft, and precipitate dews, so that the isles not only have a rich soil which is excellent for planting, and also produce a natural fruit that is plentiful and wholesome enough to feed without toil or trouble, a leisured folk."

Also: "where the air was never extreme, which for rain had a little silver dew, which of itself and without labor, bore all pleasant fruits to their happy dwellers." [Plutarch, Life of Sertorius, ch. viii]

Elysium does not have any animals or horses and cattle, except birds. Jinns do not eat meat, apart from the meat of fish. Their diet comprises fruits, pastries and fish.

The first Jinns created were possibly six in number; males and females. Two of these were the parents of Iblis who is a second generation Jinn. Jinns are of three races: Manor, Aiber and the Na'vi. Manors are light-skinned (Caucasian), Aiber, Ebony and the Na'vi, Indo-Asian complexion. Iblis comes from the Manor race. They have different color of hair that includes blue and red; as well as larger ears, with a distinct tip at the end. This tip does not protrude as sharply as may be depicted by some. It is not the pointy Elfish ear portrayed in popular media.

Jinns live a leisurely life, free of toil. They possess non-human abilities which they employ in their daily lives. They spend their time playing games and sport or general merry-making, drinking or dancing.

Creation

Angels/Jinns, Men and animals are all mostly sublime creation. We generally do not see deformed cattle or livestock amongst the billions given birth to each year. This attests to God's sublime greatness. Even the wild animals are generally free of frailties. This is a cause of puzzlement to me as I wonder why there is so much disease and deformity among humanity. The extreme multitude of diseases now common among Men is a cause for doubt and questions. These questions are important, and the thesis of this work touches on this.

It makes little or no sense to most of us when a baby is born deformed or why a child lasts little more than four years or a number of months, weeks or even days – even in an age of advanced medical practice. The incidence of disease and the suffering that accompanies it is both overwhelming and bewildering. Jinns do not suffer from this hardship.

These trends have in fact led many to doubt in God's existence or in His compassion.

Adam & "Original Sin"

The Original Sin concept has served as explanation for much of the woes we suffer and as justification for the harsh economic conditions, albeit the abundance of resources on earth.

Today's system of remuneration that is incommensurate to the amount of work put in, is now perhaps more severe than it has ever been.

We were told by religious institutions that we suffer because our ancestors, Adam and Eve sinned. Even though this failed to hold logic, it was trumpeted down the throats of generation after generation, in order to forestall revolutions. At the end we became fully indoctrinated.

The excesses of the few, who either in greed or evil hold back the earth's blessings from its masses has reached a point when many, awakened to these harsh realities reject the informal slavery decorated in the guise of jobs – jobs which bring mental, physical and spiritual misery to many. The result of this could very well be a global revolution, affecting the whole world.

Knowing fully the inevitability of this, the perpetrators of this harsh economy would now establish a control/coercive apparatus with loyalists, compliant to their wishes.

The king in Europe or the Middle East has increasingly in this latter age bonded with the ruling elite in other parts of the world, all initiated by various means and institutions into the ruling family of the world.

Sustenance

The rains that fall each year replenish the earth. Technology now available should have further eased the process by which we acquire our livelihood.

There is constant talk about population and the land available to us. This is truly astounding when you consider the amount of land on earth. There is talk of a need to depopulate the earth. Would God in this vast world create Men and not provide land and sustenance for them. Why is this happening? Seven billion people if they come together standing, would not occupy more than the city of Rome. I would therefore think that seven billion people would very much inhabit the country of Italy – less land for farming and livelihood.

For those who deny God, it is good evidence for believing in the future end of the world (earth life), since an ever reproducing population would eventually run out of space and resources – and with no clearly habitable planet discovered in space, most likely perish.

Reptiles

Reptiles are a species that I have both loathed and questioned all my life. I consider reptiles alien to our world before 2297 BCE. I believe that every man hates snakes and I see it as one way to know a man from an alien.

No man would ever want to come into bodily contact with a snake. This is not just out of fear for its bite but also because of an internal revulsion within us. If this is how you feel, then sure enough you are a man and not an alien to our world.

You see, it is not illogical to assume that one created world has crossed into our side of the world by some means, and is now upsetting the balance our world, including its livelihood – depriving masses.

It is of note that some men now refer to Reptilian Bloodlines whom they blame for the greed, gluttony and subjugation we now experience. These are not some Space beings however. They are "Gog & Magog".

Unfortunately, these men also appear to suffer from Darwinism and the instruments designed and employed long ago to prevent or make it difficult, if not impossible for us to discover their origins or source. Monotheist religion and those who preached the faith gave us a lot but we mostly have turned away from this – considering it archaic and devoid of real progress. What we fail to see is that these men were neither idlers nor power hungry tyrants.

You find yourself on earth with parents who, if not for these men would not tell you anything beyond the fact that they begot you. You ignore a belief in God or the Angels and embrace a belief that your great-grandfather was a monkey, when over 1400 years ago the Qur'an revealed that some men were transformed into apes – i.e. way before Darwin corrupted the world with his theory of Evolution. Yet, the history of those whom these theorists learned from is steeped in mysticism and 'philosophy'.

My friend, if the messages of the Prophets were difficult to believe yesterday, it is no longer the case today. Forget the invented Monasticism that now ravages even Islam; there is a lot to use and much that was revealed. There is also much to live for.

"Race toward forgiveness from your Lord; and a Garden whose expanse is like the expanse of the heaven and earth; prepared for those who believe in God and His messengers." [Qur'an 57:21]

You may look up the universe and read about Blobs which are connected by filaments and taking up vast portions of Space. You can also find information on clouds containing 'alcohol' – enough for billions to consume over billions of years. The Qur'an mentions wine in Paradise.

Yeshua (Jesus) and Muhammad

Original Sin & Atonement is the belief that Adam's Sin is forgiven with the descent to earth and death on the Cross of Jesus Christ. That, by his death, all mankind having faith in Jesus Christ is forgiven.

The often confusing piece of this doctrine is identifying the person of Jesus. Was Jesus God, or was he a son of God? The latter is often difficult to place since Monotheist faiths, under which Christianity is categorized, do not propound a doctrine of two gods. If Jesus were the son of God, this would mean he is divine and therefore a deity next to God.

If we take the line that God came to the earth to die for our sins, we would be left with the question of whether God can die. Can divinity die?

The second thesis is of a son of God that came down to the earth to die for our sins.

The Bible makes mention of Jesus sitting on the right hand of God and as narrated, we are told he prayed to God while in distress (indicating a second person).

If we say this person was sent to die for our sins so that we may be forgiven – freeing us by this act, of a stiff requirement of deeds (works of righteousness) and leaving us with the easy route to salvation through faith in him, we are presented with the following questions:

- Who forgives sins?
- Why suffer yourself or someone else just for you to forgive that person or persons? Was something owed to another being or beings?
- Is God not the most forgiving of all who forgive?

I always thought it was for God to forgive and that repentance was often enough.

Is it being supposed that the enemies of Adam and his progeny were being appeased?

If that is the case, Satan sinned when he disobeyed God and sinned again when he whispered into the heart of Eve. Is God answerable to anyone? That is impossible.

If we are to say that this act compensated for Adam's sin, what about Adam's punishment when he was sent down to the earth.

Again, any man can go through the ordeal Jesus is said to have gone through and many men had suffered like this in unjust rulings. There were for instance two other men next to him on the cross.

Are we to think that God or 'his son' had to suffer and be nailed to a cross, in order for God to forgive us? Makes any sense? Well, this was the departure from the Monotheism that men were sent to teach.

The Qur'an says: "Blessed is He in whose hand is dominion; who, created death and life to test you, (as to) which of you is best in deed. And He is the Exalted in Might, the Forgiving. [Qur'an 67:1-2]

The doctrinal precedence of faith over works has helped spoil our world, since it is our actions that make up the world we live in.

Islam is simply, submission to God. Islam is the religion taught and practiced by all the prophets.

Jesus for example, practiced what was practiced by the Israelites. He did not build a Church or introduce a new form of worship. He went to the Synagogue like others, and never in the Bible called his followers a new name.

Was Noah a Jew? The answer is no. Was Lot a Jew? Again, the answer is no. This is beautifully put in the Qur'an.

"Abraham was not a Jew or Christian but he was one inclined toward truth, a Muslim (one who submits to God). And he was not of the Polytheists." [Qur'an 3: 64-67]

Judaism began after Moses, and Abraham came before Moses. These men (prophets) principally preached one message: God is one God, and He alone is God. Alongside this they exhorted one another to good deeds. Nations came out of some of them, like the Israelites from Jacob.

Although the evidences are obscure, Joseph found a good leader in Egypt, who was in all likelihood a Monotheist. Would a pagan Pharaoh make a Monotheist like Joseph who would have practiced devoutly his religion, governor and deputy in the land? Were these Monotheist Egyptians converted by Joseph? I wouldn't think so. They were Monotheists who believed in one God, 'Amun'.

Judaism is based on the Torah and the Talmud.

Islam therefore is the name given to the religion practiced from Adam to Muhammad, and the meaning of the name holistically covers all features of the faiths practiced by all Monotheists throughout history. Muhammad did not introduce a new religion. He simply claimed to have been called by the One God to call all men to Him and remind them.

Some find it difficult to believe that a prophet emerged from amongst the Arabs as if they too are not special to God.

The Messiah

The Messiah was the person sent by God to guide the Jews and bring hope to the world.

We, Muslims, believe that this person was Jesus, or better put, Yeshua (the name in Hebrew) and Isa in the Qur'an. Some have come to believe that he is God's son, but how can this be so if having a son would require a wife; and God hath no wife.

"Originator of the heavens and the earth, how could He have a son when He does not have a companion? Created He all things and He is of all things knowing. That is for you, God, your Lord. There is no god but He. Created He, everything; then worship ye Him. And He is Disposer over all things. [Qur'an 6:101-102]

In coming to earth, Yeshua was to try to help a nation that was under threat of corruption and misguidance – and were specifically targeted by Satan. They were now a nation that rejected messengers sent to them and rather held obedience toward Pharisees and others instead of prophets like John (Yahya) who had come before Yeshua. They even killed or attempt to kill these Messengers; like in the case of Yeshua and the beheading of John. They seemed drawn away from God and now strayed from the Path.

Yeshua was therefore sent to re-establish this nation on the Guidance. But most importantly he brought signs (wonders) that would answer any doubt in the supreme being of God and the truth of the revelations, at a time when this and other nations were under the control and influence of a pagan 'Greco-Roman' empire.

Who is Yeshua?

Yeshua is neither Man, nor Angel, God or a son of God. He is a Spirit-like being who is the first creation of God. He may be the 'Ruuh' (Holy Spirit).

At a time when these pagan Roman powers ruled vast territories of the inhabited world, bringing their cults, dying-and-rising deities and beliefs to a large area of the world, this being was sent to re-establish the faith of the Israelites and other good, patient men. Resurrection was no longer the wondrous promise held in faith by Men, to be a deed promised by God at the end of the world.

The Greeks, well before the Romans had begun propagating this with plausible success in that part of the world.

This would therefore have been a matter of profound inquiry in the minds of Believers, and would have tempted some into embracing the paganism of the day, since the greatest cautioner i.e. death would have seemed of no serious consequence.

The information on Greco-Roman religion is relatively scant due to the common loss of information over time and other factors. Yet, we shall manage with what survives for the purposes of this treatise.

The much trumpeted death and resurrection of Jesus pales in light of these preceding rites. But his teachings and the reminder he brought, especially when combined with the miracles he performed would have renewed the hopes and faith of many, besides the obstinate.

A list of the miracles performed by Yeshua in the Apocrypha Gospels and the Qur'an include the under listed:

1. Molding from clay the form of a bird and giving it life by breathing on it
2. Curing the blind
3. Curing the lepers
4. Raising a dead man to life
5. Providing food miraculously in response to a request by his disciples (The Last Supper)

Some of the Israelites accepted him as true, and as the Messiah. Others however, conspired against him.

I have found no clear verse in the Bible where Jesus says he is God, calls himself the 'son of God' or one verse where he asks men to worship him.

Yeshua did not die. Rather, he was taken up by God. In the Qur'an it is said that it was made to appear like this to them.

Yeshua's followers were persecuted severely after his departure. You may look up the Early Followers of Jesus. The last of those who still clung to some of the original teachings of Jesus Christ were Arius and his followers, whose total demise began around 325 CE when Christianity was given its first official recognition in the Roman Empire. This is approximately 300 years after Jesus.

As per the canonical Gospels, the earliest record of these dates around 100 CE. With the earliest followers of Yeshua being Hebrew, one would expect to have a Gospel in Hebrew. No Gospel in Hebrew survives.

It is better for every man to worship one God as this is what was preached by all the prophets. Secondly, there can be no mistake in that. The Qur'an tells us: "Do not say three. Say One."

The beauty about this is that you cannot possibly err if you stick to a faith in one. If you consider more than one God, then it is possible that one might not be God. It is purity, as you cannot be wrong when you believe in only one God.

Muhammad

Muhammad was a man of exemplary character. He was kind, charitable, modest, trustworthy, patient and even shy. At the time of his prophet hood the Arabs were possibly the most lagged of the nations with much cruelty persisting in their society. You may say he was the Humanitarian of the age, concerned about the poor and oppressed, and unconvinced about the idolatry and polytheism of that time.

Since all the prophets were of exemplary character, Muhammad emerged distinct from the rest of his kinsfolk when he received a message and mission from God to go against the Polytheism and ignorance of the time and propagate the belief in one God, righteous living and justice for all.

This radical mission was equally successful, and the Arabs would champion the right of Monotheism over the centuries. In marked completion of his mission, the Arabs were elevated across the ages, bringing enlightenment and civilization to many nations.

The man himself led a simple, austere and modest life, establishing the honor of all the prophets and messengers sent by God – and setting up the system for the glorification of God.

It is therefore totally puzzling that the Jewish and Christian establishments having rejected him have sought to portray him as a pseudo prophet. It was through Muhammad that the chastity and truth of Maryam (Miriam) was confirmed since the Jews do not to date believe Jesus to be the Messiah or believe in his virgin birth. The reasons for these attacks are twofold:

1. Islam is the world's purest practice of Monotheism
2. The Anti-Christ would find it difficult to deceive men if most of the world was Muslim

The message of Islam is simple. It is to believe in and worship only one God whilst performing good deeds. It is avoiding the sacrilege of Satan who seeks to set himself up as partner to God, whilst seeking to fulfill his vow to subjugate Men.

Controversies

Westerners often attack Muhammad's marrying multiple wives but this should not be of consequence since other prophets like Jacob, David, Solomon, etc had multiple wives.

They attack his choice of marrying Aisha, but she was at least fifteen. Marrying someone at that age was common in those times.

Perchance, the most common attack is on the wars fought. As per this, other prophets like David fought wars in their time. What is to note is that the enemy would not have allowed for Islam to take root. His followers were persecuted and killed.

Even when he migrated to Medina, the Pagans of Mecca pursued him there to put an end to the growth of Islam. It was the Pagans who travelled on more than one occasion to fight the Muslims. Crucially, it must be said that his conduct of war was exemplary. He did not fight the man who did not fight him or attack women and children.

What the enemy resolved to do was to suppress and by any means annihilate the growth of Islam, like was done to the early followers of Jesus.

The Qur'an commands: "Let there be no compulsion in religion" [Qur'an 2:256]. Therefore, the assumption that Muslims spread Islam by the sword must be false. That Muslims expanded their territory cannot be denied. In the context of those times, I find it hard to accept that this would have been avoidable. This may be discussed in a separate treatise. However, the current insurgencies and wars being waged by some, in the name of Islam, apart from the struggle in Palestine, lack legitimacy.

It has been counter-productive to a guided Muslim nation and the hearts and minds of Men. I consider these acts of internal/external sabotage that now threaten the Islamic edifice and message.

Muhammad's relationship with the Jews was difficult. Some Jews did embrace the message but many did not. The Muslims were often locked in conflict with the Jews, when treaties or pacts were not honored by them. The reasons for this and that difficult-to-understand question of the Jew will be uncovered in this book.

Muhammad left us with an incorruptible Qur'an that is not only sublime in form but could not have originated with a man or woman.

His teachings as narrated in ahadith have not remained intact and free of corruption. But we can make some breakthrough with a good amount of his teachings.

Anti-Christ: Age of the Anti-Christ

The name Muslims have for the Anti-Christ is "Dajjal". "Dajjal" may mean 'False Messiah' [not able to save or deliver those whom he would wish to deliver] or 'Deceiver'. He is called "the one-eyed Deceiver".

The "Dajjal", contrary to portrayals as having only one eye, is not literally one-eyed. He possesses two eyes but has an abnormality in one of his eyes; the right eye. His right eye is described as bulging out like a grape. The eye of the "Dajjal" is significant.

He is further described as young, with ruddy complexion, and as sturdily built with cropped hair.

Some of the signs before his appearance are as follows:

- Many people would worship Satan
- People will mortgage their faith for worldly gain
- Dishonesty will be the way of life
- Falsehood will become virtue
- Interest will become legitimate
- There will be little or no shame amongst the people

- There will be little or no respect for Elderly people

It is narrated from Muhammad that: "Between the creation of Adam and the coming of the Last Hour, there will be no tribulation more serious than the tribulation of the False Messiah (Dajjal). It is also narrated that he will be of Jewish descent.

Iblis

Iblis is the name (given name) apart from Satan, in the Qur'an, for the enemy of Man. He is today known by other names, including Zeus, Jupiter or Odin. It is common knowledge among some that he has two wives; Freya and Frigg in Norse mythology. One of these is his mother, who is of the first generation. Yes, Iblis is the outlaw. He married his mother, Cybele (also; Rhea, Hera or Ceres).

His second wife is from the third generation of Jinns. Diana/Artemis is likely this second wife. There is a story of a "Broadcaster" with two wives. This is his story. The name 'Broadcaster' may refer to his promiscuous ways. Cybele is generally portrayed as fat, whilst Diana is shown as slender.

Iblis is also Odin in Norse mythology who sacrificed his eye in exchange for a mystical drink. In those myths two wives are ascribed to him, together with a favorite son, Thor. It is this son, Thor that is the Anti-Christ.

In the 111th chapter of the Qur'an, there is mention of one "Abu Lahab" (means; Father of Flame), who many have incorrectly called, an uncle of Muhammad. "Abu Lahab" (Father of Flame) is Satan.

Who is the Anti-Christ (False Messiah)?

As already noted, the False Messiah is one of the sons of Satan. He has appeared in ancient pagan religions as Ares (Roman; Mars), Heracles/Hercules and Norse; Thor, from whose name Thursday is derived.

Statue of Ares [Ares Ludovisi Altemps]

Ares, literally meaning "Battle" was the Greek god of War. The Greeks were ambivalent toward Ares. Although he embodied physical valor necessary for success in war, he was overwhelmingly insatiable in battle, destructive and man-slaughtering. [Burkhert, Greek Religion, p.169] The counter-part of Ares among the Roman pantheon was Mars. Human sacrifices were offered to Ares in Sparta.

In Rome, Mars' festivals were held in March (named for him) and in October, which began the season for military campaigning and ended the season for farming. The Norse, Thor, was associated with strength, hallowing and oak trees. In the records of the Germanic peoples by the Roman historians, Thor is frequently referred to as Hercules.

The False Messiah is the chosen one of the enemy. Based on many clear evidences, we can say that we now live in the time of the False Messiah. The world is manifestly ready with the aid of technology for this individual to begin his mission. Descriptions of the "Dajjal" (False Messiah), travelling, like the clouds (aero plane) or that you will be able to hear him at once all over the world (radio), indicate this. The False Messiah is from the nation of Gog and Magog.

It is this nation that paved the way for his coming, employing a host of means.

They have operated from the shadows – recognizing each other and collaborating covertly; an advantage which has facilitated most of their schemes, as they instigate wars – alongside this, achieving greater control and goals. Their mission can be glimpsed in bits here and there – never once exposing its entire agenda, producing remarkable cover stories, explanations and historical accounts. Research in order to expose them is nearly impossible if not guided by God.

As the time approaches for the final phase of their plans and the preponderance of details amass, some individuals have managed snippets which are yet difficult to add up.

David Icke for instance, noticing some weird facts among some prominent personalities like the Royal Family attempted to explain these abnormalities. This body of scholars have given the term; "Reptilian Bloodlines" to these people. The problem though is that many seek to explain these phenomena with mainly, if not totally, information that originates from them, or the sciences taught in schools.

We should however thank them for their work, knowing the unpopularity of such attempts. We know the systematic disparaging and disposal established by them via the media, organizations and institutions etc.

I have used religious, scientific and philosophical sources, together with fables to piece together this treatise.

The Anti-Christ and his fellowship seek to equate themselves with God. Some of the clearest references to this include the great magic which we now see performed. At times it is not even referred to as magic.

I recall an instance on stage in 2010 when Stevie Wonder (music artist) was told he would be given his baby voice again with the ingestion of a liquid, at the Glastonbury festival; and was told not to call it magic. True to what was offered, it worked. But Stevie called it magic and so the gift was withdrawn. At that same festival, I witnessed on television someone swallowing a short sword.

Beyond what I have mentioned, you may have witnessed the performance of even greater feats that cannot be explained by our physical laws or that totally defeats logic. What may be the only thing left to witness is a resurrection of the dead. This could very well not be too far along.

The term False Messiah describes a being that even though able to perform great feats lacks authenticity – either owing to the process by which he achieved such powers or the inability to truly save. Clearly, one does not have to go through missions or make extreme, unspeakable sacrifices in order to attain such powers. In the case of Yeshua, he simply, by God's permission brought the dead to life and after molding from clay a bird, gave it life with his breath.

The Jews rejected the true messiah, Yeshua. As a result, they still wait for the first coming of the Messiah. Consequently, when the False Messiah comes to them, most if not all, will embrace him as that – especially since they are the only one of the Monotheistic faiths to have suffered the most devastating infiltration of Gog & Magog. Their religion has become a mostly 'Kabbalist' faith full of isolated practices. Perhaps it is why it is barely open to the rest of humanity.

Gog & Magog and Cyrus 'the great'

Ezekiel 38, 39

1. The word of the Lord came to me: Son of man set your face against Gog & Magog ... the chief prince of Meshek and Tubal.
21. I will summon a sword against Gog on all my mountains, declares the Sovereign Lord. Every man's sword will be against his brother.
22. I will execute judgment on him with plague and bloodshed; I will pour down torrents of rain, hailstones and sulfur on him and on his troops, and on the many nations with him.
23. And so I will show my greatness and holiness, and I will make myself known in the sight of many nations. Then they will know that I am the Lord.

39:7 I will no longer let my name be profaned...

1. For seven months, the Israelites will be burying them in order to cleanse the land.

Gog & Magog (folklore)

According to a poem: In the 3970th year of the creation of the world, a king of Greece married his thirty daughters into royalty, but the haughty brides colluded to eliminate their husbands... The youngest would not be a party to the crime, and so divulged the plot, so that the other princesses were confined to an un-steerable, rudderless ship and set adrift. After three days, they arrived in England. [Barber 2004]

Images of Gog and Magog (depicted as giants) are carried by Lord Mayors of the City of London in the Lord Mayor's Show, each year on the second Saturday of November.

In the prelude to the 2003 invasion of Iraq, George Bush told Jacques Chirac that Gog and Magog were at work in the Middle East: "This confrontation is willed by God" …"who wants us to use this conflict to erase his people's enemies before a New Age begins. [Block (2012) p.151]

Gog & Magog in the Qur'an

"Then he followed a way. Until when he reached (a pass) between two mountains, he found beside them a people who could hardly understand (his) speech.

They said, O Dhul Qarnain (Cyrus), indeed Gog and Magog are (great) corrupters in the land. So, may we assign for you expenditure that you might make between us and them a barrier?

He said: that in which my Lord has established me is better, but assist me with strength (manpower); I will make between you and them a dam.

Bring me bars of iron – until when he had leveled (them) between the two mountain walls, he said: Blow (with bellows). Until when he had made it (like) fire, he said; Bring me that I may pour over it molten copper."

So, they (Gog & Magog) were not able to scale it, nor were they able to effect in it any penetration.

(Dhul Qarnain) said: This is a mercy from my Lord; but when the promise of my Lord approaches, He will make it level, and ever is the promise of my Lord true." [Qur'an 18: 92-98]

Muhammad, in a narration by Ali bin Abi Talib described them as people with long hair, large ears, broad faced (faces like shields) and with sharp canine teeth, who copulate like donkeys. They are also said to consume everything they come across. These narrations are crucial in identifying Gog & Magog among mankind.

The name, Gog & Magog refers to the progenitors of the Gog & Magog nation. It is also used to refer to the nations which emerged out of them.

Gog & Magog and their progeny can be found amongst mankind today, but this was not originally so. They emerged among humanity around 2297 years BCE, and have lived alongside the progeny of Adam from this period to date – approximately 4313 years. At the time the prophecies recorded in Ezekiel 38 & 39 were revealed, Gog & Magog would have spread among the many nations of the earth, and to the north of Europe. They would have introduced new languages, culture and even technology to those areas.

This book primarily seeks to identify Gog & Magog, their origins and motives.

I believe without doubt that Cyrus 'the great' was Dhul Qarnain. Cyrus was also a Monotheist.

His freeing of the Jews from captivity in Babylon, and his aid of the reconstruction of the house of worship in Jerusalem are perhaps the only indications left to prove this fact, amidst dogged efforts to designate him a Polytheist. No Polytheist in history has come close to mimicking such exemplary and remarkable conduct and dispensation – within the influence of great conquests. Not even Alexander, the Macedonian may equal him. Any avid student of history would be able to identify the Monotheist in Cyrus with ease.

Cyrus' conquests helped slow the advances of Gog & Magog and ameliorate the conditions of the masses of men enduring life at this time. The conquest of Babylon probably overthrew a Gog & Magog state. Gog & Magog do not waste time in usurping thrones and resent living under Man-led governments. Following, I shall refer to them as Humans and to the original inhabitants of earth as Men.

Babylon holds a story with a few important connotations. Some Jews it was reported approached Muhammad, who later received revelation about what was inquired of him. They appear to be probing for details and it appears that what was revealed was restricted in its information. The verses relate:

"Or have you thought the Companions of the Cave and the Inscription, a wonder among Our signs? (Mention) when the youths retreated to the cave and said, Our Lord grant us from Thy Self mercy and prepare for us from our affair right guidance.

So, We cast (a cover of sleep) over their ears within the cave for a number of years. Then We awakened them that We might show which of the two factions was most precise in calculating what (extent) they had remained in time…

And We bound (made firm) their hearts when they stood up and said: Our Lord is the Lord of the heavens and the earth. Never will we invoke besides Him any deity. (If we do) we would have certainly spoken, then an excessive transgression. These, our people have taken besides Him deities. Why do they not bring for (worship of) them a clear evidence? And who is more just than one who invents about God a lie?

(The youths said to one another), when you have withdrawn from them and that which they worship other than God, retreat to the cave. Your Lord will spread out for you of His mercy and prepare for you from your affair facility… And they remained in their cave for three hundred years and exceeded by nine. [Qur'an 18]

The number who retreated to the cave is not given.

I believe that this incident took place in Babylon and that it refers to Daniel and those with him.

The 'Inscription' was likely the famous "Writing on the Wall" event, interpreted by Daniel and foretelling the end of the pagan Babylonian state.

The number of those who retreated to the cave would have been many – judging by the verse which mentions the youths talking to one another (as if covertly passing messages around).

Apparently, there were those from Daniel's own people, who shockingly to Daniel and his companions had embraced the Polytheism of the state. They appear extremely touched by the apostasy of 'their own people' – indicating that these were likely Gog & Magog among the Israelites (something that may be proven when we come to the tribe of Dan).

The lack of clear evidence for embracing this polytheism astonishes the youths – indicating that those who promote and proclaim paganism or corruption are commonly Gog &

Magog, like we shall see in Livy's account. The identity of Gog & Magog apparently remains hidden to the youths.

From the east to the frontiers of Egypt, Gog & Magog would have been in control. They would have acquired this by marriage into royalty – as men were not the snubs we now see, who do not intermarry with the common people. This practice of inter-marriage among royalty today, of course goes back a considerable period in history and is obviously one of the examples of leadership i.e. alien to the people – which preserves bloodlines that are united by a common agenda across the ages.

Dhul Qarnain (Cyrus) was empowered by God to halt the progress of Gog & Magog and retake most, if not all of the states under their rule – apart from Egypt which was the last to fall to them (under Cleopatra in 50 or 51 BCE, who conspired with the Romans).

The usurping of thrones was mainly achieved through marriage. They employed any and whatsoever means to marry one of their women into a ruling family. This addition to the family would give birth to one of theirs who would conspire or collaborate to gain accession to power by covert and treacherous means, peaceful or violent. Many such instances can be found in history. Gog & Magog are today a part of every race.

They are those who reincarnate after dying. The process by which they come into our world and their continuous reincarnation will be exposed with supporting evidences. They are distinguished from the rest of men but these may pass with little or no notice.

The third canine tooth on both the left and right upper rows of the teeth is sharply pointed. Their ears are often different; protruding outwards, as you may notice in the picture below. Third, there is sometimes a slight, dark patch around their eyes if you look keenly, as if suffering from insufficient blood. For those who may want to connote this as alluding to hate for any part of humanity, I would again like to remind you that they are among every race. My brother may be one of them.

Consider the movie, "Sleeping with the Enemy". "Sleeping with the Enemy" is a 1991 psychological thriller film in which a woman escapes from her abusive husband who is described as obsessed with organizing his cupboards and hand towels. Try to see if this fits you. Are you, if in your twenties or older, particular about tidiness?

There are reports of concentration camps being constructed by FEMA in the US and huge increases being made to Storm Troopers. There are also reports by some unconventional politicians about houses being marked, using different colors. These are worrisome trends in light of what I now present.

Sample of someone from the nations of Gog & Magog

In any case, Gog & Magog were halted in their progress by Cyrus 'the great (Dhul Qarnain). In a location in present day Hungary, Cyrus, as part of his efforts to constrain them constructs the dam mentioned in the chapter of the Qur'an. This dam came down in 2010.

The people of this region were men who suffered perhaps from frequent raiding on their cattle and wealth by people of the Gog & Magog nation who would have migrated further north or populated among the peoples up north. The nations of Gog & Magog would have at first struggled to fend for their livelihood like men since Jinns are not used to work. Yes, they are originally Jinns who have become incarnate into our world. This is what Reptilian bloodline theorists who suggest that they are Space beings, have failed to grasp.

A narration regarding the Anti-Christ calls him a Jinn – but this narration has enjoyed little support from the Islamic scholarship; most of whom are from the Gog & Magog nation. It is why they refrain from calling the age what it is; and refuse to discuss Gog & Magog or acknowledge that all we now wait for is the end of the world.

Coming across this piece of news in Danish newspaper, Jyllands-Posten that the CIA paid an Al-Qaeda spy $250,000 to help find a bride for American-born Anwar Al-Awlaki in a plot to locate and kill him was significant. Awlaki was clearly misguided about the challenges we face, by these infiltrators who disguise their way into positions among every community. As a result, his response was extreme and wrong. The bride was obviously one from Gog & Magog; used to deceive and wreak havoc. Men like him choose a wife carefully. It would only have been their perennial existence in our communities that would have made something like this possible.

When Cyrus of Persia defeated Croesus of Lydia in the middle of the 6th century BCE, Miletus fell under Persian rule. In 499 BCE, Miletus' tyrant, Aristagoras became the leader of the Ionian revolt against the Persians. Persia quashed this rebellion and punished Miletus by selling all of the women and children into slavery, killing the men and expelling all of the young men as eunuchs. A year later, Phrynicus produced the tragedy, "The Capture of Miletus" in Athens. The Athenians fined him for reminding them of their loss.

Miletus was originally inhabited by the Leleges who were driven out by the Dorian invasion (a Gog & Magog nation). Herodotus (1.171) says that the Leleges were a people, who in old times dwelt in the Aegean region – and that they were driven from their homes by the Dorians and Ionians. After this, they took refuge in Caria, and were named Carians. Gog & Magog are self-aware. They know themselves and each other.

Ever wondered why you are ganged upon in social situations or why it is difficult to fit in? In any case, you (the man) are the one trying to understand this treatise. If you would like an easier life, try to identify those fitting their physical description around you so that you can make true friends. Another of their features is a wider forehead. As you may struggle to make out their teeth (above), try focusing on the entire face; on the forehead, teeth, ears, right eye etc.

Homosexuality is another of their characteristics. I am not trying to say that it is an exclusive trait of 'Humans' (**hued out of man**).

The reason for Homosexuality amongst them is because a male Jinn's spirit becomes incarnate into the body of a female and vice versa. Human females scarcely ever marry men. In most cases, they only marry a man for his wealth or some other benefit. A union of this kind is often turbulent.

Male Jinns in a female body tend to marry men since they find it difficult to attract spouses from their own kind. They may appear masculine in physique or behavior, big-butted and scarcely good looking.

Pelasgus: The Pelasgians; Danaids, Dorians and Archaeans; Arcadians

Dionysos is the first Human. He was born in 2297 BCE. He was not born of a woman (progeny of Adam) but was in part (biological) of Adam.

His conception, incubation and delivery heralded the first artificial insemination and delivery of a human in the world, and would be celebrated among many cultures – even to date. Zeus, employing artifice slept with a woman, "Semele", in the guise of her husband. Being a woman, and thus incompatible with Jinn, Semele miscarried. The fetal discharge would prove useful for the insemination into the womb of Cybele, who ultimately delivered the child, Dionysos.

The account in Greek mythology is close. The child that was born is the progenitor of all Humans (Gog & Magog) on earth. This human being was Zeus first human incarnation on earth. The intricate process involved allows for the Jinn to exist in his world as Jinn and in our world as a human. It involves a division of the spirit (life). During his development in the womb, one part of his spirit is stored in a rock (Philosopher's Stone). At birth, this spirit joins with the child. Without the spirit, the child delivered would be a zombie or 'total retard'.

Dionysos, being part man, would be compatible with women. This is the story of Zeus-incarnate. In order for him to reproduce, other Jinns would have to undergo the process, providing spirits for incarnation.

Upon death, the spirit in the human body returns to the rock, where it remains for twelve days – to be incarnated on its 13th day. It does not exceed the thirteenth day, or the spirit would be lost. Should there be no ready child to receive the spirit, it incarnates into a 'modified' animal.

This story is tied to the story of Rhea's conception of Zeus, who she took to the island of Crete (Knossos], where the infant Zeus grew up in the cave of Ida. It is the same story.

When I first read the story, I questioned why the location was in our world. Part of this deceiving narrative is that it was to save Zeus from his infant-devouring father.

Dionysos is the father of Pelasgus. In Greek history, Pelasgus was the eponymous ancestor of the Pelasgians who established the worship of the Dodonaean Zeus around 2000 BCE.

In the different parts of the country once occupied by the Pelasgians, there existed different traditions as to the origin and connection of Pelasgus. The Ancient Greeks even used to believe that he was "the First 'Man.'"

The problem faced is that the authorship and recording of history is managed by the ones we attempt to expose.

Pelasgians

The Pelasgians as the name reveals were the descendants of Pelasgus, who was the first male descendant of Dionysos. Historically, the Pelasgians were regarded as a Sea-faring nation. Sea-faring as a lifestyle of the nations which emerged from Dionysos is ubiquitous, appearing to be the case also with the tribe of Dan, the disputed tribe of Israel. They probably used this means for their livelihood; fishing, raiding, piracy and expansion.

Raiding villages and towns was one main aspect of the life of the Vikings for instance. It would have served as an effective means for escape – and a reliable means for unleashing surprise attacks. Moreover, it would have complemented their small numbers when you consider that they only emerged around 2297 BCE.

The most plausible reason, yet, is that owing to the lifestyle of Jinns who did not work or farm in Elysium and Atlantis etc, they would have found it difficult to fend for themselves like Men. A lifestyle of raiding with the aid of ships would have as such been the prevalent option.

Populations identified as Pelasgian spoke a language that at the time Greeks considered as barbaric. The areas they occupied generally fell within the ethnic domain that by the 5th century BCE was attributed to those speakers of ancient Greek, identified as Ionians.

"Until when he reached (a pass) between two mountains, he found beside them a people who could hardly understand (his) speech. [Qur'an 18: 93]

The verse could be understood to reveal the following:

- That Cyrus had travelled to an area much influenced by the language or dialect of Gog & Magog.
- That at this initial phase Persia and the regions surrounding Persia were not subsumed into their language
- That the men in Asia Minor and Persia were not distant in language

Gog & Magog are used to introducing their language or languages. This aids interpersonal communication among them and enables a technical concealment system in literature and ancient records that is largely comprehensible to them.

Ionic Greek (Standard Greek)

The Ionic dialect appears to have originally spread from the Greek mainland, across the Aegean, at the time of the Dorian invasions, around the 11th century BCE.

By the end of the Greek Dark ages in the 5th century BCE, the central west coast of Asia Minor, along with the islands of Chios and Samos, formed the heartland of Ionia proper. The dialect was soon spread by Ionian colonization to areas in the northern Aegean, the Black Sea and the western Mediterranean. The Ionic dialect is generally divided into two major time periods; Old Ionic (or Old Ionian) and New Ionic (or New Ionian).

The works of Homer (the Iliad, the Odyssey and the Homeric Hymns), and of Hesiod were written in a literary dialect called Homeric Greek or Epic Greek, which largely comprises old Ionic, with some borrowings from the neighboring "Aeolic" dialect to the north.

Ionic acquired prestige among Greek speakers because of its association with the language by Homer, and the close linguistic relationship with the Attic dialect, as spoken in Athens.

This was further enhanced by the Writing Reform implemented in Athens in 403 BCE, when the old Attic alphabet was replaced by the Ionic alphabet. This alphabet eventually became the standard Greek alphabet; it's use becoming uniform during the "Koine era". It was the alphabet used in the Christian Gospels and the Book of Acts.

Argives

The name Argives comes from Argos. Argos was continuously inhabited as a substantial village for the past 7000 years. [Avelender. Douglas J, (2010) Eventful Archaeologies: New Approaches to Social Transformation in the Archaeological Record]

Argos was colonized by Pelasgian Greeks around 1100 BCE.

The Achaeans

The Achaeans and Arcadians were in my opinion Men who were the original inhabitants of Greece.

The Achaeans were the inhabitants of the region of Achaea – a region in the north-central part of the Peloponnese. The term was originally given to those Greeks inhabiting Argolis and Laconia. I believe that Argolis is their original territory.

Pausanias and Herodotus both recount that the Achaeans were forced from their homelands by the Dorians, during the Dorian invasion of the Peloponnese. It was then that they moved into the region called Achaea. Eduard-Meyer supports the assertion that the real-life Achaeans were mainland pre-Dorian Greeks. The Achaeans spoke Aeolic Greek.

Hellenes

The Hellenes are modern-day Achaeans. They are native to Greece, Cyprus, Southern Italy and Turkey. According to many historians the Proto-Greeks (Pelasgians: Argives, Danaids etc) probably arrived in the area now called Greece, in the southern tip of the Balkan peninsula, at the end of the 3rd millennium BCE. [Cadogan & Langdon Caskey (1986) p.125]

The sequence of migrations into the Greek mainland during the 2nd millennium BCE has to be reconstructed on the basis of ancient Greek dialects, as they presented themselves centuries later – and are therefore subject to some uncertainties. ["The Greeks" – Encyclopedia Britannia]

Dodona

Dodona was the oldest oracle, dating to the 2nd millennium BCE according to Herodotus. The earliest accounts describe Dodona as an oracle of Zeus. It was considered second only to the oracle of Delphi in prestige. The oracle was first under the control of the Thesprotians before it passed into the hands of the Molossians.

According to Nicholas Hammond, Dodona was an oracle devoted to Rhea, but called 'Dione', who was joined with Zeus. [Hammond (1986) p.39]

According to Strabo, the oracle was founded by the "Pelasgi" [Strabo, Geography 7.7]

By now, it should have started becoming apparent that the paganism of ancient Greece came with the descendants of Pelasgus. The oracle at Dodona is the oldest, and it was established in the second millennium BCE. At its earliest, it would not have exceeded 2297 BCE. This is supported by Pindar who called Zeus, a Pelasgian. [Strabo. Geography]

To assume therefore, that all of the ancient Greeks practiced this polytheism is incorrect. This is what we have been led to believe, but Plato for example was both a Man and a Monotheist as is evident in his works.

Bust of Plato

In Plato's "Lecture on the Good", he identifies "the Good" with the One. More can be found in Plato's "The Forms", where he says: The Forms are the cause of the essence in everything else, and the One is the cause of it in the Forms. [Metaphysics 988]

It was the Pelasgians who reintroduced paganism to most of the world. The world was flooded because of Paganism, and the men who succeeded learnt this lesson.

The Pelasgians (also, Denyen) sought for centuries to colonize Egypt but failed. Successive Pharaohs repelled their attacks and even carried out pre-emptive strikes on them. In the Papyrus Harris I document, there is a document which reads: "I slew the Denyen in their isles and burned the Tjekker and Peleset."

Pandora: Rhesus factor [Avatars]

There are four main Blood groups; O, A, B and AB. The blood in most of these contains a protein known as the RhD (Rhesus factor). If this is present in your blood, you are classified as RhD positive. 85% of world population is RhD positive.

If this is not present in your blood, you are classified as RhD negative. 15% of world population is classified as RhD negative.

Applying the Rhesus factor to our blood grouping produces eight categories:

- A RhD positive (A+)
- A RhD negative (A-)
- B RhD positive (B+)
- B RhD negative (B-)
- O RhD positive (O+)
- O Rhd negative (O-)
- AB RhD positive (AB+)
- AB RhD negative (AB-)

An estimated 85% of the UK population is RhD positive. Similarly, 85% of world population is considered RhD positive.

RhD factor emerged from a gene shared with the Rhesus monkey, which it is named after. Rh Blood types were discovered in 1940 Karl Landsteiner and Alexander Wiener. This was forty years after Landsteiner had discovered ABO – Blood groups.

The Rh factor can lead to serious medical complications between a mother and fetus. Mother-fetus incompatibility occurs when the mother is Rh- and her fetus is Rh+. Maternal anti-bodies can cross into the placenta and destroy fetal red blood cells.

Rh type mother-fetus incompatibility occurs when an Rh+ man fathers a child with an Rh- mother. When both the mother and the fetus are Rh negative (Rh-), the birth will be normal.

Rhesus disease is a condition where anti-bodies in a pregnant mother's blood destroy her baby's blood cells. It is also called hemolytic disease of the fetus. Rhesus disease doesn't harm the mother, but it can make the baby anemic or jaundiced. It can lead to still-birth, brain damage, learning difficulties, deafness and blindness.

In the previous chapter, I detailed Dionysos' conception and birth. It is from Dionysos that the world became populated with people who differ in gene and DNA. 'Humans' are in my view, those who make up the Rh-negative part of population.

Artificial insemination as a means of conception is now well known today. If this were the 1700s, it would have been completely implausible to advance this. The process by which the very first human was born into our world can be described as 'Artificial insemination'.

The story as it is in Greek mythology narrates how Zeus planted the fetus into his testicles.

It is this that was inseminated into Cybele (Rhea), mother and wife of Zeus.

Pregnant Cybele depicted giving birth on her throne which has two feline-headed hand rests

That child being part of a woman would exist in our world and not the world of the Jinn. Cybele, as such, serves primarily as the 'incubating vessel' and channel of delivery.

Triple-stranded DNA is a DNA structure in which three oligonucleotides wind around each other, forming a triple helix.

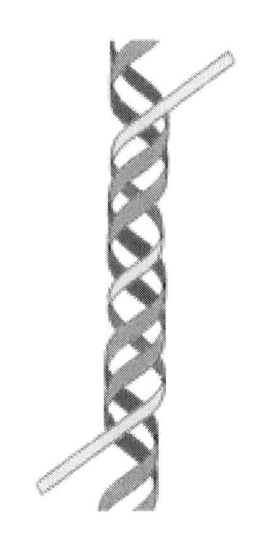

Triple-helix DNA

Double-stranded DNA or Deoxyribonucleic acid is the more common of DNA types, consisting of two biopolymer strands coiled around each other to form a double helix. These strands contain nucleotides.

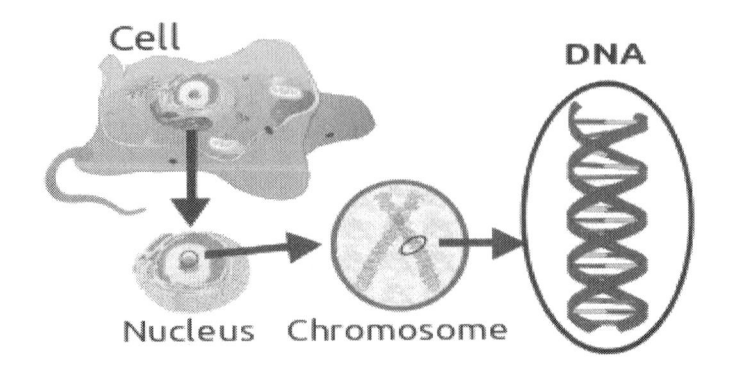

Eukaryote DNA

Deoxyribonucleic acid (DNA) is a molecule that carries most of the genetic instructions used in the development, functioning and reproduction of all living things. Humans are of different DNA and as well differ in gene.

Avatar

In Hinduism, an Avatar is the human of animal form of a Hindu god on earth. An avatar is typically the incarnation of a deity in earthly form. The original word, "Avatarati" means "he crosses over".

Pandora

The story of Pandora is a Greek tale about the first woman created by Zeus. According to the legend Pandora was created to punish men for the fire which Prometheus gave men.

On examining this legend, you will see that it is simply an allegory for the presence of Humans (chiefly, the female) among Men. Pandora may well have been the first female Human and the punishment part is very much likely an allusion to the beginning of suffering unleashed by the female Human on Men. See: "Sleeping with the Enemy" (movie).

Hesiod recounts: "From her is the race of women and female kind: of her is the **deadly** race and **tribe** of women who live amongst **mortal** men to their great trouble, no help mates in hateful poverty, but only in wealth." [Hesiod's Works and Days, 590-593]

I am sure that most men in their thirties upwards can make up the rest. The Pandora woman is that archetypal female who strangely causes you hurt you cannot understand.

Pythagoras

Throughout my research, one personality stands out; revealing proofs about the Incarnates.

Pythagoras is said to have claimed that he had existed as Euphorbus, the son of Panthus in the Trojan War and as a tradesman and another time, a **courtesan,** in other periods.[Porphyry Vit. Pyth. 26, Diogenes Laertius viii-5, Pausanias ii-17]

This is one confirmation of the view premise on birth-death and returning to life.

According to Xenophanes, Pythagoras heard the cry of his dead friend in the bark of a dog. [Diogenes Laertius viii.36]

In his book, The Life of Appollonius of Tyana; Philostratus wrote that Pythagoras knew just not who he was himself, but who he had been. [Flavius Philostratus, Life of Appollonius of Tyana, Vol.2, Book vi]

Heraclides Ponticus reported that Pythagoras claimed four previous lives which he remembered in detail. [Diogenes Laertius, viii 3-4] One of these past lives according to Aulus Gellius was as a beautiful courtesan. [Aulus Gellius, iv. 11]

"To prove his Phyrgian existence, he was taken to the temple of Hera, in Argos, and asked to point out the shield of the son of Panthos – which he did without hesitation. [E. Cobham Brewer (1894) Dictionary of Phrase and Fable (PDF) p.1233]

Another personality like Pythagoras was Socrates. Consider the assertions of Pythagoras that he could recount his previous lives. This would mean being knowledgeable on many matters if all the information recollected is accumulated. Now, consider Socrates, who in several dialogues advances the idea that knowledge is a matter of recollection, and not learning and observation – implying that it is not empirical.

This would designate the present exhibition of especially scientific knowledge, fraudulent. Socrates is found arguing that knowledge is not empirical, and that it comes from 'divine' insight. [Baird & Kaufman, 2008] "He who sees with his eye is blind" – Socrates

Socrates argues with Plato regarding some of these beliefs.

In Meno, Socrates uses a Geometrical example to argue that knowledge is acquired by recollection. He cites a geometrical construction by an illiterate slave boy, who could not in common instance have known how to do this. The knowledge must be present, Socrates concludes. The slave boy would have been a human like Socrates.

Pythagoras' life as a courtesan goes to support the premise on homosexuality.

Plato classified people into three categories:

- Productive: Laborers, carpenters, plumbers, masons, merchants, farmers, ranchers etc. which correspond to the appetite part of the soul.
- Protective (Warriors or Guardians): adventurous, strong or brave; in the armed forces, which correspond to the spirit part of the soul
- Governing (Rulers or Philosopher kings): intelligent, rational, self-controlled, in love with wisdom, well-suited to make decisions for the community who correspond with the reason part of the soul.

The "Protective" category makes me worry. This is because humans make up the vast majority of the coercive and law enforcement authorities.

Incarnation

Incarnation literally means embodied in flesh or taking on flesh.

Gilgul (Kabbalah) describes a Kabbalist concept of reincarnation. In Hebrew, the word 'Gilgul' means cycle or wheel. Souls are seen to cycle through lives or incarnations, being attached to different bodies over time.

The concept relates to the wider process of history in Kabbalah, involving Cosmic Tikkun (Messianic rectification) and the historical dynamic of ascending lights and descending vessels from generation to generation.

The Caduceus

U S Army Medical Corps plaque

The caduceus symbol associated with medicine is one striking example that suggests how much humans know about DNA and how aware they are of their kind. Notice the wings at the top.

A caduceus is a short staff entwined by two snakes. As noted before, I believe that snakes were not created by God. You may ask if not only God creates. Yes, only God creates. These corrupters bring about different animals and forms from what God had already fully created. I suggest that snakes were brought about from human blood by a process of alchemy.

To support this assertion, I would like to propose the cloning and breeding of animals. The vast species of dog today were bred by these humans.

Another topic to note is the uncontrollably rampant existence of diseases and deformities now prevalent in the world. You may have already deduced correctly that this was brought about by the incarnation of Jinns among us.

On the subject of diseases, useful may be Plato's suggestion in the Republic that not everyone is disposed to be Health practitioners.

Dionysian Mysteries [Attis & Cybele]

Cybele is Phrygia's only known goddess. Her Phyrgian cult was adopted and adapted by Greek colonists across Asia Minor. It spread from there to mainland Greece and its more distant western colonies.

In Greece, Cybele was assimilated into her Minoan equivalent Rhea.

Many of her Greek cults included rites to a divine Phyrgian castrate shepherd- consort, Attis.

Attis was consort of Cybele, and the two were honored in cults with eunuch priests ('Galli'). The story of Attis recorded by the traveler, Pausanias, has some distinctly non-Greek elements.

There is a story related about an Agdistis who initially bore both male and female attributes. The Olympian gods, fearing Agdistis, cut off the male organ and cast it away. There grew up from it an almond tree, and when its fruit was ripe, Nana, a daughter of the river god Sangarius picked an almond and laid it on her bosom. The almond disappeared and she became pregnant. Nana abandoned the baby, Attis. [Pausanias. Greece 7, 19]

Statue of a reclining Attis at the Shrine of Attis

In Rome, Cybele was known as "Magna Mater" (Great Mother). With Rome's eventual hegemony over the Mediterranean world, Romanized forms of Cybele's cults spread throughout the Roman Empire.

At Pessinos in Phyrgia, the mother-goddess took the form of an unshaped stone of black meteoric iron. [Summers in Lane (1996) p.364]

Strabo notes that Rhea-Cybele's popular rites in Athens were held in conjunction with Dionysos' procession. Like Dionysos, Cybele was regarded as having a distinctly un-Hellenic temperament, simultaneously embraced and held at arm's length. Cybele was the focus of the first mystery cult. This cult had private rites with a chthonic aspect connected to hero cults, and exclusive to those who had undergone initiation. [Roller (1999) .225-227]

Reliefs show her alongside young female and male attendants with torches and vessels for purification. Literary sources describe joyous abandonment to the loud, percussive music of tympanon, castanets, clashing cymbals and flutes. Cybele was associated with various male demi gods who served as attendants, and with dactyls and magicians. Cybele's major narratives attach to her relationship with Attis, who is described by ancient Greek and Roman sources and cults as her youthful consort, and as a Phyrgian deity.

A 4th century Greek Steele shows Attis sporting the Phyrgian cap and shepherd's crook of his Greek and Roman cults.

Attis Thymiaterion Louvre

Attis accompanied the diffusion of Cybele's cult through Magna Graecia (Greater Greece). In the mid 2nd century, letters from the King of Pergamum to Cybele's shrine at Pessinos consistently address its chief priest as Attis.

Cybele fountain in Madrid, Spain

Romans knew Cybele as "Magna mater deorum Idaea" (Great Idaean mother of the gods). The goddess arrived in Rome in the form of a black meteorite stone.

Lucretius vividly described the procession's armed war dancers in their three-plumed helmets, clashing their shields together, bronze on bronze, delighted by blood ; yellow robed, long haired, perfumed "Galli" (priests) waving their knives, wild music of thrumming tympanons and shrill flutes. Along the route, rose petals were scattered and clouds of incense arose. [Summers in Lane]

Holy Week in March

The holy week for Cybele and Attis began in the Ides of March to about the end of the month. Citizens and freedmen were allowed limited forms of participation in rites pertaining to the mysteries, through their membership of two colleges; each dedicated to a specific task; the "Cannophores" (Reed Bearers) and the "Dendrophores" (Tree Bearers).

- March 15: Canna Intrat (the reed enters), marking the birth of Attis and his exposure in the reeds along the river Sangarius where he was discovered by shepherds. The reed was gathered and carried by the Cannophores.
- March 22: Arbor Intrat (the tree enters), commemorating the death of Attis under a Pine tree. The Dendrophores (tree bearers) cut down a pine tree and suspended from it an image of Attis, carrying it to the temple with lamentations. A three-day period of mourning followed.[Forsythe, Time in Religion p.88]
- March 23: On the Tubilustrium, a holiday to Mars, the tree was laid to rest at the temple of the magna mater.
- March 24: (Sanguem or Dies Sanguinis – Day of Blood) a frenzy of mourning when the devotees whipped themselves to sprinkle the altars and effigy of Attis with their blood; some performed self-

castrations of the Galli (priests). The holy night followed with Attis placed in his ritual tomb.
- March 25: (Vernal equinox on the Roman calendar): "Hilaria" – Rejoicing, when Attis was born.
- March 26: Requietio (Day of Rest)

After all this, Cybele's sacred Stone was taken from the Palatine temple to the Porta Capena and down the Appian Way to the stream called Almo, a tributary of the Tiber. There, the stone and sacred implements were bathed in the Phyrgian manner by a red robed priest.

- March 28: "Initium Caiani", sometimes interpreted as Initiations into the mysteries of magna mater and Attis, at the Gaianum, near the Phyrgianum sanctuary at the Vatican Hill [Salzman. On Roman Time, p.165, 167]

Citizens who sought initiation into her Mysteries could offer either of two forms of bloody animal sacrifice – and sometimes both as lawful substitute for self-castration. The "Taurobolium" sacrificed a bull and the "Cribolium", a ram.

A priest stands in a pit beneath slats of wood. His assistants dispatch a bull using a spear. The priest emerges from the pit drenched in the bull's blood. [Beard, p.172] The testicles of the bull were offered as sacrifice. "The celebrant personally and symbolically took the place of Attis, and like him was cleansed, renewed, or in emerging from the pit or tomb, reborn. [Duthony, p.119]

These regenerative effects were thought to fade over time, but they could be renewed by further sacrifice. Some dedications transfer the regenerative power of the sacrifice to non-participants, including emperors and the imperial family. Some mark a "Dies Natalis" (birthday or anniversary) for the participant. Dedicants and participants were male or female. [Duthony, p. 69, 101-104, 107, 115]

Dionysian Mysteries

The Dionysian Mysteries materialized between 3000 and 1000 BCE. The Dionysian Mysteries are not predated by any other cult. The cultivation of wine came under the lore of Dionysos.

The mysteries had an atavistic component and focused much on life-death cycles. They emerged from Minoan Crete.

The basic principle beneath the original initiations, other than the seasonal death-rebirth theme, supposedly common to all vegetation cults was one of spirit possession and atavism.

The spirit possession involved the invocation of spirits and communal dancing to drum and pipe with characteristic movements (such as the backward head flick) found in all trance inducing cults (reprented most famously today by African "Voodou").

As in Vodoun rites, certain drum rhythms were associated with the trance state. This is detailed in Greek prose, particularly the Bacchae of Euripides.

"Following the torches as they dipped and swayed in the darkness, they climbed mountain paths with head thrown back and eyes glazed, dancing to the beat of the drum which stirred their blood…In the state of "ekstasis" or "enquosiasmos" they abandoned themselves…At that moment of intense rapture, they became identified with the god himself." [Hoyle. Peter, (1967) "Delphi"] According to some reports, the participants even transformed into animals – a thing, some say was made possible by chthonic powers.

This practice is preserved by the rite of the "goat and panther men" of the heretical "Aissaoua" Sufi cult of North Africa.

The most desired possession was that of Dionysos himself. Commentators view this as hardly discernible given the primal nature of these deities. This ritualized atavism was also associated with a descent into the underworld (life in the stone, after death) of which Dionysos is believed to lord. ["Hades and Dionysos are one and the same," declared Heraclitus]

Many of its initiates tended to be slaves in Greek society, from whom its leadership was often drawn – in a typical inversion of society.

Alexander 'the great' was initiated into the cult. He spread the cult of Dionysos internationally; to Palestine, where he was identified with Adonai, of the Jews and, most far flung of all, to India – where he was identified with Shiva.

The cult became increasingly more complex and would eventually break away to form part of the Philosophical Orphic and Pythagorean Mysteries.

People today claim the precursors of Christianity, Devil worshippers and Witch covens in the Rites of Dionysos.

The main festivities of the Dionysian Mysteries were held in the month of Elaphebolion (around the time of the Spring Equinox). The festival coincided with the clearing of the wine occurring after the Winter Solstice – when it was declared Dionysos was reborn. This was formalized to January 6 (now Epiphany); a day in which water turned to wine. A rite known as the "Dance of the Fiery Stars" was performed. It appears to be appropriation of the dead; which was continued in Christian countries as "All Souls Day".

Another rite mentioned involved hunting animals (this would represent Dionysos) and eating them raw. Orphic versions of the Dionysiac mysteries include the dismemberment by the Titans of the young Dionysos who has first transformed into a bull, and his resurrection as a second Dionysos.

In the Eleusinian Mysteries Dionysos was mourned for a whole year (his death) as Dionysos Chthonios (lord of the Underworld) and in the whole of the second year was celebrated – supposed to be his resurrection as Dionysos Bacchus. That is, the year during which Dionysos was in the womb was a period of mourning. The next year in which he was celebrated would mark his life and period of living.

The initiate at the end of the process is usually said to have become a Bacchus. He is shown the contents of the Liknon and presented with the thyrsus wand.

"Over all reigned the Phallus, which in its symbolism, a rebours – represented post- ejaculation; the death state of Bacchus, the god of pleasure, and his resurrection when it was in 'forma errecta'. Of such was the sorrow and of such the joy of the Mysteries" [White. A E, New Encyclopedia of Freemasonry]

Bacchanalia

Bacchanalia was the Roman form of the Mysteries. Livy offered an account of the cult associated with frenzied rites, sexually violent initiations of both sexes, and the cult as a murderous instrument of conspiracy against the state.

In the Bacchanalia mysteries, the priests held the duty of revealing sacred things and represented the demiurges (creator). The torch-bearers went by the name of "Lampadophores", their chief personifying the sun. Processions featured vessels with wine that was covered with vine branches. Participants (hierophants) marched one and along singing the "Phallica", obscene songs in honor of Dionysos.

In the rear of this motley crowd came the "Phallophores" and "Hyphalli", the former exhibiting shamelessly to the spectators, images of the 'lingam' which by means of straps were tied to the hip, and the latter carrying the same objects, but of more gigantic dimensions, at the end of a long pole.

The title, Magna Mater deorum Idaea is important to note in this chapter. Also to note are the Stone of Cybele (meteoric rock), thyrsus (wand) and blood from castration. Cybele's title is not shared by any other pagan deity. She is the mother of Zeus, who married her son, and a major accomplice and partner to the mischief wrought by Satan. She is also a major progenitor to Jinns as noted before.

Crete, the island where she delivered the infant Dionysos (see; birthplace of Zeus by Rhea) was probably a largely uninhabited place during this period. Zeus (i.e. Dionysos) would probably have had only animals as neighbors and Cybele/Rhea as carers. Crete may well be where Greek paganism originated, spreading to other parts of Asia Minor and mainland Greece.

The fact of Dionysos (Zeus) birth and upbringing in the cave of Ida may be reinforced by the rumor around 600 BCE that Zeus was buried in Crete.

"They fashioned a tomb for thee, O holy and high one – the Cretans always liars, evil beasts, idle bellies! But thou are not dead: thou lives and abides forever. For in thee, we live and move, and have our being. [Epimenides Cretica]

In the apotheosis of Melicertes and Leucothea, Cyprian says: "The cave of Jupiter (Zeus) is to be seen in Crete, and his sepulcher is shown." Commentators note that Zeus was being confounded with Dionysos.

To suggest that Crete (note the word; cradle) was previously uninhabited or largely uninhabited would hold, since it is an island. The place of Crete in history is mostly surrounded by the Minotaur (Bull-man) story and the Labyrinth. This story is possibly unshared by any other nation in the history of the world.

The idea of a woman copulating with a beast is both savage and extreme. Something like this would only be done by a desperate folk (i.e. humans). My mother or anyone's sister would not partake in such an act; neither would a man ask this of his wife or daughter.

Greco-Roman Paganism: Titans & Olympians
[Ceres-Liber-Libera]

In the ancient Greek and Roman religion, the Twelve Olympians are the major deities of the Greek pantheon. "Pantheon" (from Greek) means literally "a temple of gods."

Statue of Diana/Artemis/Libera [Diane de Versailles]

They are generally listed as Zeus, Hera, Artemis, Poseidon, Demeter, Athena, Apollo, Ares, Hephaestus, Hermes, Aphrodite and Pluto.

According to Pindar and Herodorus, their cult was established by Heracles.

It happens that these Olympians are presented as an alternative to Monotheism, and their cults believed to be suppressed by adherents of Monotheism, with attempts to revive and establish these practices once again.

Having mentioned Zeus (Iblis) as the son of Rhea/Hera (Cybele) and her consort, it is logical to see him as a Titan. Since the children of progenitors form the masses and enjoy the advantage of numbers, it is rubbish to think there was a fight between the progenitors and their children.

The story of the Fight was likely just another insinuation portraying that Oneness as domineering and overly restraining. The entity, Saturn (Cronus), as related is supposed to be the father of Zeus. Zeus' father by the way is Prometheus; the original mate of Rhea (Cybele) who was tricked by her to turn into a bee – following which she swallowed him.

Saturn was often associated with the old, the former. To understand some of the background we need to look at Saturn.

Saturn

Saturn is a deity in ancient Roman religion. Saturn is a complex figure because of his multiple associations and long history. He is generally accepted as the first deity of the Roman Capitol. The period during which Saturn was worshipped is regarded to have been the Age of plenty and peace. Men were said to have enjoyed the spontaneous bounty of the earth without labor, in the Golden Age described by Hesiod and Ovid.

In December, he was celebrated at what was perhaps the most famous of the Roman festivals, the Saturnalia; a time of feasting, free speech, gift-giving and revelry.

Saturn's name appears in the ancient hymn of the 'Salian' priests.

With Saturn, we see how, in one part of the world (southern Italy), a deity, perhaps 'the One', was worshipped. Most striking is the description; "Golden Age," used to refer to this time. It is in direct contrast to the hard life men and women now endure and an indication that humans brought misery to our world.

An in-depth look at Saturn reveals some commonalities with God in Monotheism. Most of what is recorded appears to be derisive of this being. Saturn is a pre-Greek deity in southern Italy.

Finding useful resources on Saturn is difficult but it would help any research on proving that the world before 2297

BCE was chiefly Monotheist. Cronus is the name the Greeks gave to Saturn.

The Pelasgians, upon their arrival in southern Italy would have brought the name Cronus as their name for Saturn and through their domination and presence in the arts and recording of history would have corrupted the identity of the entity, Saturn.

The propaganda espoused is to a large extent identifiable in their concept of Saturn and as well their political and social philosophy. Their clamor for freedom and doing away with the former is all the more apparent today. This would have impacted on the psyche of previous generations and raised questions in them – just as it has with us.

Their 'overbearing' portrayal of Saturn as the restrained or strict all the more makes it difficult not to assume that this is the God in the Old Testament. Their imprint is apparent with the attribution of a spouse to the deity – just like they did with Amun of the Egyptians. These Olympians are no more than Jinns whose mission is to free themselves from any form of subordination whilst enjoying themselves to the fullest. The following verse in the Qur'an gives us a clue:

"And they have made between Him and the Jinn a lineage. But the Jinn have already known that they (who make such claims) will be brought to punishment." [Qur'an 37: 158]

Possibly, it is to prove their subservience that they were put under the command of Suleiman (Solomon) as revealed in the Qur'an. They served as helpers in the construction of the house of worship in Jerusalem, in various capacities. [Qur'an 27]

The echoed shouts for freedom suggest these entities are demanding a freedom that includes even being free from God.

"I will create a skin (Bashar) out of clay, from an altered black mud. And when I have proportioned him and breathed into him of My Spirit, then fall down to him in prostration.

Hence, the angels prostrated – all of them entirely, except Iblis (Satan); he refused to be with those who prostrated.

(God said) O Iblis, what is (the matter) with you that you are not with those who prostrate? He said, "Never would I prostrate to a man who you created out of clay from an altered black mud.

(God said) Then depart from it, for certainly you are expelled. And certainly, upon you is the curse until the Day of Recompense.

He said, My Lord give me respite until the day they are resurrected.

(God said) Then indeed you are of those given respite until the day of the time well known." [Qur'an 15: 29-38]

You may doubt in God in view of their rebellion or the times we live in. The next verse may help you find strength. Do not be deceived by what seems obtainable today.

"Surely, Satan is an enemy to you – so take him as an enemy. He only invites his party to be among the companions of the Fire." [Qur'an 35: 6]

Satan cleverly convinced his kind into believing there is a way out. This is partly why incarnation into our world takes place. By some 'alliance' with beings that they never knew existed, the Jinns were deceived.

"Then, do those who disbelieve think that they can take My servants instead of Me as allies?" [Qur'an 18: 102]

Note that the word describing the allies is "servants". As Satan and those with him are rebellious and do not worship God, it rules them out as being the allies here referred to. Hence, it is not men seeking out Satan and his cohorts as allies to support them in some ploy; rather it is Satan and his cohorts seeking out other beings as allies. These supposed allies are "the Loa" in chapter eleven.

Ceres-Liber-Libera

Ceres, Liber and Libera, together form the Aventine or Eleusinian triad. Some modern historians describe the Aventine triad as a Plebian parallel to the Capitoline establishment after the Plebian tribunes gained increasing influence over Rome's religious life and government.

Ceres

Ceres, an equivalent of Rhea, was depicted in art with a scepter, a basket of flowers and fruit, and a garland made of wheat ears. The word cereal derives from Ceres. The name Ceres comes from the Indo-European root, "Ker" meaning "to grow" which is also the root for the words 'create' and 'increase'.

Libera

Libera was a goddess of wine, fertility and freedom. She, together with Ceres were paired with Liber (Free Father), Roman god of wine, male fertility and guardian of Plebian freedoms as triadic cult companion in a temple established on the Aventine Hill (ca. 493 BCE). Libera and Ceres are the wives of Liber.

Liber

In ancient Roman religion, Liber (the free one) or Liber Pater (the free father) was a god of viticulture, wine, fertility and freedom.

In ancient Lavinium, he was a phallic deity who championed freedom as opposed to dependent servitude.

Livy gives an account of the Bacchanalia's introduction by a foreign soothsayer, a Greek, of mean condition. "The cult spreads in secret like a plague. The lower classes, Plebeians, women, the young, morally weak and effeminate males ("men like women") are particularly susceptible: all such persons have "levitas animi" (fickle or uneducated minds), but even Rome's elite are not immune."

The Bacchanalia's priestesses urge their deluded flock to break all social and sexual boundaries, even to visit ritual murder on those who oppose them or betray their secrets [Sarolta. Takacs, (2008) Vestal Virgins, Sibyls and matrons: Women in Roman Religion]

The cult was officially represented as the workings of a secret, illicit state within the Roman state, a conspiracy of priestesses and misfits, capable of anything.

Note that all these cults are interrelated. Liber's "Liberalia" festivities which were jointly held with the Bacchanalia in March were moved to April as Ceres' "Cerelia" of April. According to Cicero, Liber is the son of Ceres. Liber's role in viticulture and winemaking is complementary to Jupiter's (Liber is Jupiter).

He personified male procreative power which was ejaculated as the "soft seed" of human and animal semen. His temple held the image of a phallus. In Lavinium, this was the principal focus of his month-long festival, when according to Augustine, the "dishonorable member' was placed on a trolley and taken in procession around the local **crossroad shrines**. [Cambridge Texts in the History of Political Thought]

It is important to note Livy's description of "effeminate men" in his account on the Bacchanalia. This supports my assertion that an intrinsic female being is born into our world into a male body, and an intrinsic male being into the body of a female. It is within this that the concept of the Hermaphrodite is contained.

Hermaphroditus

Myths: Jason and the Argonauts

Jason and the Argonauts are the ultimate ending to a task which first began with Hercules and the Twelve Labors. His Labors were the preparation to his completion of what started way back amidst the effort of Jinns to attain independence from God.

Consider what David Ulansey said about the Mithraic Mysteries which according to him began in the Greco-Roman world as a religious response to the discovery by the Greek astronomer, Hipparchus of the astronomical phenomenon of the procession of the Equinoxes – a discovery that the entire cosmos was moving in a hitherto unknown way. He suggests that this cosmic motion was seen by the founders of Mithraism as indicating the existence of a powerful new god capable of shifting the cosmic spheres and thereby controlling the universe. [Ulansey. D, Origins of the Mithraic Mysteries]

Hercules completed the Twelve Labors. This final part of his effort is not, as it may appear, one adventure, lasting at most a few years – but in fact one that began thousands of years ago, lasting up to 2010 (CE).

We will come to know whether or not they were successful. I am sure they weren't.

The location of the place where the Argonauts emerged is somewhere around the country of Georgia in Europe. The "Two Seas" mentioned are likely the Two Seas mentioned in the Qur'an.

"And Mention when Moses said to his boy: I will not cease (travelling) until I reach the junction of the Two Seas or continue for a long period. [Qur'an 18: 60]

This would be the junction between two worlds – one of which is our world. The Two Seas are the sea of the Jinn world and the sea of the world of Men. The fish in the oceans swim between the oceans of both worlds. One type of fish, the Tuna fish is not advisable to eat. This fish has undergone some form of alteration by the Jinns and is as such quite possibly harmful to men.

In the story, Aetees, who possessed the Golden Fleece is most likely not a man. He would be from among the "Loa" presented in the next chapter. The Fleece itself is not some ordinary object. It may be the Holy Grail, much adored in literature and the history books. The Holy Grail brings with it a dominion and independence.

Jason, by obtaining it would have given his father a dominion; 72% of Space.

In Book Two of Appollonius Rhodius' "Argonautica", the Argonauts arrive in the land of Phineus. There, they are told about the "Clashing Rocks" where the "Two Seas" meet – which no one had before them won an escape between.

"First of all, after leaving me, ye will see the twin Cyanean rocks where the two seas meet. No one, I ween, has won his escape between them…First entrust the attempt to a dove when ye have sent her forth from the ship. And if she escapes safe with her wings between the rocks to the open sea, then no more do ye refrain from the path, but grip your oars well in your hands and cleave the sea's narrow strait...But if she flies onward and perishes midway, then do ye turn back; for its better to yield to the **immortals.** For ye could not escape an evil doom from the rocks, not even if Argo were of iron."

On towards, the Argo eventually sailed between the Clashing Rocks.

The "Argonautica" Book Three mentions the scheming of Athena to make Medea, daughter of Aetees, (possessor of the Golden Fleece) fall in love with Jason in the hope she would help him obtain the Fleece.

Jason, after meeting with Aetees, requested of him the Fleece – to which Aetees replied: "Stranger, why needest thou go through thy tale to the end? For if ye are in truth of heavenly race, or have come in wise inferior to me, to win the goods of strangers, I will give the Fleece to bear away, if thou dost wish, when I have tried thee…Two bulls with feet of bronze I have that pasture on the plains of Ares…I cast into the furrows of the seed, not the corn of Demeter, but the teeth of a dreaded serpent that grow up into the fashion of armed men; then I slay at once cutting them down beneath my spear as they rise against me on all sides…If thou wilt accomplish such deeds as these, on that very day thou shalt carry off the Fleece to the king's palace…For indeed it is unseemly that a brave man should yield to a coward."

"Thus he spake; and Jason fixing his eyes on the ground, sat just as he was, speechless, helpless in evil plight. For a long time he turned the matter this way and that, and could now take on him the task with courage."

"At last, he made reply with crafty words: With thy plea of right, Aetees, thou dost shut me in over, much. Wherefore also I will dare that contest, monstrous as it is, though it may be my doom to die. For nothing will fall upon me more dread than dire necessity, which indeed constrain me to come hither at a king's command."

On Jason's return to the Argo, he is addressed by Argus: "Son of Aeson (Jason), thou wilt despise the counsel which I tell thee, but, though in evil plight, it is not fitting to forbear from the trial…If we could win her aid (Medea), there will be no dread, me thinks, of thy defeat in the contest; **but terribly do I fear that my mother will not take this task**

upon her. Nevertheless I will go back to entreat her, for a common destruction overhangs us all."

The story continues that they were helped by the daughter of Aetees, who fell in love with Jason. This is though contradicted by other sources like the Athenian Vase paintings, where his helper is not Medea but instead, Athena.

Jason, with the help of Medea, eventually steals the Golden Fleece and makes away with it. But this is again contradicted by some accounts.

On the kylix painted by Douris ca. 480-470 BCE, Jason is being disgorged from the mouth of the dragon; a detail that does not fit easily into these literary sources. Behind the dragon, the fleece hangs from an apple tree.

Jason and the Argonauts are clearly not normal men, but they interface with our world. You may observe where Aetees says: "For if ye are in truth of heavenly race" and where Argus proposes to entreat his mother (Athena). Considering what Argus told Jason, we may arrive at the conclusion that Jason and the Argonauts were relatives of at least some of the Olympians. Aetees himself, when we look at the acts he says he performs could not have been a man.

The statement of Aetees to Jason (above) seems to question a claim of being of heavenly race. This yet, confirms a claim of perhaps, divinity on the part of Jason. All this, put together reveals fraudulent claims and deceit when we look at the words of Phineus who says: "But if she flies onward and perishes midway, then do ye turn back; for its better to yield to the **immortals**" – indicating fraudulent claims of immortality on the part of these Olympians and their cohorts.

Here, the immortals mentioned would not have been the "Olympian deities" since not one of them appears to be against Jason and his mission. As a matter of fact, Jason and the Argonauts enjoyed their help and support.

The task which Aetees presents to Jason leaves him completely overwhelmed and forlorn – appearing unskilled for the task. Their only hope is Medea, who, forget the 'susceptible female cliché is in fact one of the "Loa". As I understand it she even loathed the guy. As such the only option was to steal the Fleece. According to the "Argonautica" the Golden Fleece was eventually stolen.

The Jinns who followed Satan, gambled their lives away, and are now left with fire as a result of their efforts. "He only invites his party to be among the Companions of the Fire." [Qur'an 35: 6]

I believe there are Jinns who now know this but have not divulged its facts – resting on useless hope.

The Loa (Divination)

The Loa [Mysteres/Invisibles] are beings that are spirit-like; also considered to be the spirits of the Voodou. They are neither Angels nor Jinns.

They were made by the "Ruuh" ('holy Spirit') and like all creation are subservient to God.

The Loa are divided into some three nations: "Rada", "Petro" and "Ghede" Loa.

Entities making up Rada Loa include, Anaisa Pye, Ayizan, Agwe, La Sirene and Erzuile Freda. They are associated with the color, white.

Ghede Loa is mostly associated with the dead and are traditionally led by Baron Samedi. The color associated with them is black. Petro Loa is associated with the color, red.

Baron Samedi is depicted with a top hat, black tail coat and dark glasses. He is shown as having a white, frequently skull-like face and or skull for a face. Baron Samedi is the Loa of resurrection. He spends most of his time in the invisible realm of spirits. His followers on occasions wear black, purple or white clothing.

As with nearly everything, the resources available on the Loa are corrupted. As per the background and nature of these beings, it is difficult to find authentic details on the Loa.

"Eloah"

The notion of divinity underwent radical changes throughout the period of early Israelite identity. The ambiguity of the term "Elohim" is the result of such changes, cast in terms of vertical translatability i.e. the re-interpretation of the gods of the earliest recalled period as the national god of 'mono-latrism', as it emerged in the 7th to 6th century BCE, during the Babylonian captivity; and further, in terms of monotheism, by the emergence of "Rabbinical Judaism" in the 2nd century CE.

"Mono-latrism" is the recognition of many gods but with the consistent worship of only one God.

It is also this development in the history of the Israelites and the worship of the one God while in captivity in Babylon that Daniel and those with him would have decried and found corruption from the original religion.

"Elohim" is a grammatically plural noun for gods in Biblical Hebrew. In modern times, it is wrongly referred to in the singular, despite the "-im" ending that indicates plural in Hebrew.

The Loa are hence joined in divinity. But the Loa are not divine. They were probably made after the creation of Man.

Aetees, in the "Argonautica" is one of the Loa. In the Qur'an we learn: "Indeed, they are planning a plan, but I have a plan. So, allow time for the Disbelievers. Leave them a while." [Qur'an 86: 15-17] For those Muslims who may want to dispute, this is another of the evidence regarding the plots of the Disbelievers, together with what is mentioned in Qur'an 18: 102.

It is from the discovery of the Loa that the Jinns joined Satan in arrogance. As noted, the Loa are the 'allies' mentioned in Qur'an 18: 102. It was from them that the Jinns learnt many things, including how to incarnate.

"Nay! Indeed 'Insan' transgresses; because he sees himself independent. Surely, to your Lord is the return." [Qur'an 96: 6-8]

Divination was to these beings that exist separately from the worlds of men and jinn. Satan (Odin) would have ultimately contacted these beings after much effort.

The story of Odin's sacrifices supports this premise. Odin undergoes sacrifices – one of which includes extracting one of his eyes as payment for a drink from the well of "Mimir" after much journeying and wandering across the world. Odin is reported to have fasted for nine days. Finally, Odin hangs, whilst he bleeds from his side for days.

All of this may be why initiation rites often involve tortuous and painful rites of passage. Odin (Satan), in his attempt to escape the Fire manages to score some pre-torment and torture, including the loss of his eye, when he should have had faith in his Lord and repented.

According to Norse religion, Odin met Mimir whose knowledge of all things was practically unparalleled among the inhabitants of the cosmos. Odin, in exchange for the water of the well gouged out his eye and dropped it into the well. Having made the sacrifice, Mimir gives him to drink water from the well. This water imparted the knowledge of the cosmos which Mimir enjoyed.

One of the narrations narrates what "the secret of Odin's doings" which Odin shared with his son, Vidar, who is described as 'the silent son'.

"To you only, O Vidar, the silent one, will I speak of the secrets of my doings. Who but you can know why I, Odin, the eldest of the gods, hung on the tree of "Ygdrassil", nine days and nine nights – mine own spear transfixing me? I hung upon that windy tree that I might learn the wisdom that would give me power in the nine worlds. On the ninth night, the Runes of wisdom appeared before mine eyes and slipping down from the tree I took them down to myself."

I do not think that things can be clearer than this. The question that comes to my mind is whether anyone would think that Men would believe in this being and take him as God, after what had come to them about God. The truth is that the humans who reside in countries like Norway shared these stories by way of their religion and beliefs. These are stories recounting the efforts made and the things achieved.

Odin goes on to say, perhaps alluding to his already incarnated self: "More, Vidar, I will tell to thee. I, living amongst Men have wed the daughter of a hero. My son shall live as a mortal amongst mortals. Sigi, his name shall be. From him shall spring heroes who will fill Valhalla, my own hall in Asgard, with heroes."

Odin appears to have spent a long time wandering around the world. This was probably in search of a way out.

"No longer was he called Odin, All-Father, but Vegtam, the Wanderer". He wore a cloak of dark blue and he carried a traveler's staff in his hands."

The Loa would certainly have been the ones who gave Odin and his loyal Jinns the apple which restores the youth of the Jinn.

The Ascended Masters

Ascended Masters or "Mahatmas" are believed to be spiritually enlightened beings who in past incarnations were ordinary humans, but who have undergone a series of spiritual transformations, originally called 'initiations'.

According to the Ascended Master Teachings, a "Master", "Commoner" or "Shaman", and as used in theology and theology terms; "Spiritual master" is a human being who has taken the Fifth Initiation, and is thereby capable of dwelling on the Sixth dimension. An Ascended master is a human being who has regained full union with his mighty "I Am Presence". This 6th stage is referred to as the "Ascension".

A "Chohan" (lord) of a "Ray" is an ascended master who has been placed in charge of one of the 12 "Rays" (until recently seven Rays were generally known, and five Rays were secret) due to having an extraordinary natural affinity of that "Ray".

A "Ray" is a concentrated stream of spiritual energy. Each ray is the embodiment/expression of one of the twelve great divine qualities such as divine-will, wisdom, love etc.

Those who have taken the seventh Initiation hold the senior administrative posts in the "Great White Brotherhood". These senior administrative posts are divided into three departments: The department of the Manu, the department of the Planetary Christ and the department of the "Mahachohan".

A lord of the world is a human being or a being of some life wave other than the human life wave who has taken the Ninth Initiation. The Ninth Initiation is the highest initiation possible on a 9D dimensional planet grid such as Earth – and it will be so until the end of the 21st December 2012.

"Sanat Kumara" ("lord of the Flame"; originally said to be from the higher dimensional planet, Venus) is the being who holds this office of the "lord of the World" here on planet earth.[The Life and Teachings of the Masters of the Far East.; King. Godfrey Ray, Unveiled Mysteries]

It is believed that he, "Sanat Kumara", is the founder of the Great White Brotherhood, which is composed of masters of the ancient wisdom (Fifth Initiation), "Chohans" and "Bhodisattvas" (Seventh Initiation), "Buddhas" (Eighth Initiation), and highly spiritually-evolved volunteers from other worlds, who have all joined together to advance spiritual evolution on earth. [Schroeder. Werner, Ascended masters and their Retreats; Ascended Master Teachings Foundation]

Theosophist, Helena Blavatsky says "Sanat Kumara" belongs to a group of beings (lords of the Flame), whom Christian tradition have misunderstood as Lucifer and the fallen angels.

Incidentally, a "father of the Flame" is mentioned in the 111th chapter of the Qur'an. It reads: "May the hands of Abu Lahab (father of the Flame) be ruined - and ruined is he. His wealth will not avail him or that which he gained. He will burn in a fire of blazing flame. And his wife – the carrier of firewood, around her neck is a rope of (twisted) fiber. [Qur'an 111: 1-5]

Guy Ballard (1878-1939) was the founder of the first "Ascended Master Teachings' in modern times, known as the "I Am" Religious Activity of the Saint Germain Foundation. The teachings were continued and embellished by later organizations such as "The Bridge to Freedom" (founded; 1951), and was known in the 1980s as the New Age Church of Christ.

The New Age Church of Christ believed that their teachings had been given to humanity by Ascended masters. These were believed to be individuals who lived in physical bodies; who had acquired the wisdom and mastery needed to become immortal and free of the cycles of re-embodiment, attaining in this way their ascension.

They considered the 'ascension' to be the complete, permanent union of the purified outer self with the "I Am Presence" – referring to the identity that is the unique individualization of God for each person. [King. Godfrey Ray, (1935) The Magic Presence, p.89]

Paganism & Catholicism

Mithras, clothed in Anatolian costume and wearing a Phyrgian cap, kneels on a bull, holding it by the nostrils with his left hand and stabbing it with his right. As he does so, he looks over his shoulder towards the figure of Sol. Two torch-bearers are on either side, dressed like Mithras; "Cautes", with his torch pointing up and "Cautopates", with his torch pointing down. [Hinnels. J R, (1976) The Iconography of Cautes and Cautopates…Journal of Mithrfaic Studies]

The event takes place in a cavern into which Mithras has carried the bull, after having hunted it, ridden it, and overwhelmed its strength. Sometimes, the cavern is surrounded by a circle, on which the twelve signs of the zodiac appear.

In some depictions, the central "Tauroctony" is framed by a series of subsidiary scenes to the left, top and right; illustrating events in the Mithras Narrative: Mithras being born from the rock, the water miracle, the hunting and riding of the bull, shaking hands with Sol, sharing a meal of bull parts with him and ascending to the heavens in a chariot.

On the specific banquet scene on the Fiano Romano relief, one of the torch-bearers points a caduceus (staff) towards the base of an altar, where flames appear to spring up. Robert Turcan has argued that since the caduceus is an aspect of mercury, and in mythology, mercury is depicted as a psycho-pomp; the eliciting of flames in this scene is referring to human souls. [Beck. Roger (2007), The Religion of the Mithras Cult in the Roman Empire]

Mithras Bull Sacrifice

Admission into the community after initiation was completed with a handshake with the 'Pater' (Father), just as Mithras and Sol shake hands. [Clauss. M, The Roman Cult of Mithras]

David Ulansey sees the cult of Mithras as important for understanding the cultural matrix out of which the Christian religion came to birth.

Dionysian Syncretism with Christianity

The word, syncretism – [Greek; "sunkretizein"] meaning to "unite against a third party" explains what I now seek to highlight.

The Christianity which originated with the Hebrews in its Monotheistic form, creed and practice threatened to spread, subsuming the Roman Empire. It thrived in Egypt, and would have appealed to Men throughout the empire.

The Roman emperors' policy was to persecute and suppress its growth for at least two and a half centuries. Around the 3rd to 4th century, when these policies no longer seemed sustainable, it compromised. It, by way of the Council of Nicaea in 325 CE began achieving what I shall term as the first major 'syncretization' of Dionysian Paganism with Christianity, in the first formal adoption and promulgation of a corrupted doctrine of a 'god-head'. It should not escape us to now note that Jesus' mission was in fact successful.

It was the increased numbers of followers of Jesus – some of whom were in the army or were prominent in the empire that forced the leadership to address the concerning challenges now posed by this religion, to the state.

I have opted to use the term, 'Dionysianism' as one encompassing term for the Paganism which started around 2200 BCE. Mithraism, Eleusinian Mysteries etc all share in the chief components of the Dionysian Mysteries; namely birth, death and rebirth. These are all just splinter cults of the Dionysian Mysteries. The level of syncretism between the Pagan beliefs and Christianity is ridiculously abundant. The similarities between this Paganism and Christianity are unexplainable. These symbols and occasions go so far as matching the death, Easter resurrection, Eucharist and celibacy of priests and priestesses. What follows are events and occasions shared by Christianity and Paganism.

- Easter Egg: Eggs were a traditional pagan symbol of fertility and rebirth. In Christianity, the egg is a symbol of the rock tomb, out of which Christ is said to have emerged to the new life of his resurrection. "The mystic Egg of Babylon, hatching the Venus Ishtar, fell from heaven to the Euphrates".
- Eucharist: The Eucharist or Holy Communion is a rite considered by most Christian Churches to be a sacrament. Christians generally recognize a special presence of Christ in this rite. Some believe that the true body and blood of Christ are really present in, with and under the bread and wine.
- The dismemberment of Dionysos by the Titans, who then eat him, can be found in the Dionysian Mysteries.
- Christmas: It was a custom of the Pagans to celebrate on the same December 25, the birthday of the Sun (Sol), during which they kindled lights of

festivity. [Mac Mullen. Ramsay, (1997) Christianity and Paganism in the Fourth to Eight Centuries]

- "Dies Natalis Solis Invicti" (meaning; the Birthday of the Unconquered Sol) was a festival inaugurated by the Roman emperor Aurelian (270-275 CE) to celebrate at the winter solstice (December 25) Christmas Day. Christmas Day is the annual festival commemorating the birth of Jesus, observed on December 25th.

- Christmas Tree: A Christmas tree is a decorated tree; usually an evergreen conifer such as pine, associated with the celebration of Christmas. In the Mysteries of Attis and Cybele, we see the "Arbor Intrat" (The Tree Enters) and the hanging of an image of Attis on a Pine tree.

- Son of god: The 'Son of god' story is present in a number of pagan religions, like the Egyptian Osiris, Isis and Horus triad. Its emergence in Christianity is shocking – considering the pure Monotheistic roots of the Hebrews.

- Lent: Lent is a religious observance that generally does not exceed the period, February to April. There is no Biblical or historical record of Christ, the apostles or the early Church participating in the Lenten season. Since there is no instruction to observe Lent in the Bible, Lent can be understood by the preponderance of pagan observations, like for example the "Holy Week in March" found in the Dionysian Mysteries.

- Shepherd's Crook & Priest/Papal attire: The Shepherd's crook now commonly depicted is associated with Attis. The Priest/Papal attire, with its cap is also similar to the images available of Attis.
- Celibacy: Celibacy is the state of voluntarily being unmarried, sexually abstinent or both; usually for religious reasons. It is often in association with the role of a religious official or devotee. In its narrow sense, the term, celibacy is applied only to those for whom the unmarried state is the result of a vow, act of renunciation or religious conviction.

    The practice of Celibacy by the Catholic Church is similar to the practice of same by the Vestal virgins and Eunuch priests of Rome.
- Halloween or All Saints Eve: Halloween or All Saints Eve is a celebration observed in many Christian nations on 31st October. It begins the three-day observance of All Hallow tide. All Hallow tide is the time in the liturgical year dedicated to remembering the dead, including saints (hallows) and all the faithful departed. It is widely believed that many of the Halloween

traditions originated from the Celtic Halloween harvest festival, "Samhain".

"Samhain/ Calan Gaeaf" marked the end of the harvest season and beginning of winter or the "darker half" of the year.

All Saints day is shared by cultures who observe a 'Festival of the Dead"

- Vatican & Massive Pagan paraphernalia: The Vatican hosts many pagan paraphernalia; from paintings to statues like the obelisk. The obelisk is a tall, narrow, tapering monument which ends with a pyramid-like top.

Vatican Obelisk in Saint Peter's Square

- Twelve Days of Christmas and Epiphany: In medieval and Tudor England, the Twelfth Night marked the end of a winter festival that started on All Hallows Eve (Halloween). The Twelve days begin on Christmas Day (December 25) and end on January 6th (Epiphany). Epiphany is a Christian holiday celebrating the revelation of 'God, the son' as a human being. In many western Christian churches, the eve of the feast is celebrated as Twelfth Night. Alternative names for the feast in Greek include "Theophany" as neuter plural and "Ta Fota", "The Day of the Lights.

Twelve Days of Christmas (Song)

On the first day of Christmas, my true love sent to me:

A partridge in a Pear tree

On the second day of Christmas, my true love sent to me:

Two turtle doves and a partridge in a Pear tree

On the third day of Christmas, my true love sent to me:

Three French hens, two turtle doves and a partridge in a Pear tree

On the fourth day of Christmas, my true love sent to me:

Four calling ("colly") birds, three French hens, two turtle doves and a partridge in a Pear tree

On the fifth day of Christmas, my true love sent to me:

Five golden rings, four calling birds, three French hens, two turtle doves and a partridge in a pear tree

On the sixth day of Christmas, my true love sent to me:

Six geese a - laying, five golden rings, four calling birds, three French Hens, two turtle doves and a partridge in a pear tree

On the seventh day of Christmas, my true love sent to me:

Seven swans a - swimming, six geese a - laying, five golden rings, four calling birds, three French hens, two turtle doves and a partridge in a pear tree

On the eighth day of Christmas, my true love sent to me:

Eight maids a - milking, seven swans a - swimming, six geese a - laying, five golden rings, four calling birds, three French hens, two turtle doves and a partridge in a pear tree

On the ninth day of Christmas, my true love sent to me:

Nine ladies dancing, eight maids a - milking, seven swans a - swimming, six geese a - laying, five golden rings, four calling birds, three French hens, two turtle doves and a partridge in a pear tree

On the tenth day of Christmas, my true love sent to me:

Ten lords a - leaping, nine ladies dancing, eight maids a - milking, seven swans a swimming, six geese a - laying, five golden rings, four calling birds, three French hens, two turtle doves and a partridge in a pear tree

On the eleventh day of Christmas, my true love sent to me:

Eleven pipers piping, ten lords a - leaping, nine ladies dancing, eight maids a - milking, seven swans a -

swimming, six geese a - laying, five golden rings, four calling birds, three French hens, two turtle doves and a partridge in a pear tree

On the twelfth day of Christmas, my true love sent to me:

Twelve drummers drumming, eleven pipers piping, ten lords a - leaping, nine ladies dancing, eight maids a - milking, seven swans a - swimming, six geese a - laying, five golden rings, four calling birds, three French hens, two turtle doves and a partridge in a pear tree

I believe this song is about the conception and incubation of Dionysos in the womb of Magna mater (great mother), Cybele and the romance between both. All of what is listed - up to the ninth month when a child is delivered is about the conception and eventual delivery of Dionysos. The eighth day of Christmas is likely referring to the eighth month of pregnancy when the pregnant woman is milking. Let us now see what someone else who considers the song to be of pagan origin and content thinks of the song and how he interprets it.

John R Henderson, author of a speculative and detective research titled, "The 12 Birds of Christmas" has given us the following.

Henderson believes that the song might be an ancient secret catechism that is centuries older than Christianity; possibly containing pre-Christian symbols linked to both numbers and birds. Presented below is Henderson's **"code to decipher the song"**.

- o A Partridge in a Pear Tree: The symbolism of the partridge comes from the fact that in the winter months, partridges leave their large flocks and form monogamous pairs.
- o Two Turtle Doves: Turtle doves have long been emblems of devoted love. But with their mournful voices, turtle doves represent both love and loss.
- o Three French Hens: The three French hens are quite simply an allusion to the goddesses in her triple forms of virgin, mother and hag. Hag was not a term of derision. It meant wise woman.
- o Four Colly Birds: The birds are really Colly Birds, not Calling Birds. Colly birds may be any of several coal-black – crows, jackdaws, rooks or ravens.
- o Five Golden Rings: They may not sound bird-like to you, but these are ringed necked pheasants. Not native to Europe, pheasants had been introduced there during Roman times…Pheasants were symbols of the element of Fire and sensuous sexuality.

- Six Geese A-laying: The important element is the "a-laying" part. The egg represents the creation cycle of birth, death, re-birth.
- Seven Swans A-Swimming: A message to celebrate the beauty of the unknown. Swans are birds of elegance and mystery. Seven represents mystery and elegance, largely in part to the movement of the seven planets (only seven were known until 1946).
- Eight Maids A-Milking: Here be eight Magpies. Magpies are black birds with milky white patches. Magpies are birds full of power and are portents used in fortune-telling...Eight magpies reminds us to put the old behind us as we start afresh. It seems significant but must be only a coincidence that by some reckoning that New Year's Day is the Eighth Day of Christmas.
- Nine Drummers Drumming: With this verse, the order of the gifts we sing is changed from the original. Instead of ladies dancing in the earliest known version, on this day drummers were drumming...The number nine represents harmony and eternity.
- Ten Pipers Piping: We sing the song the ten lords a-leaping, but originally it was ten pipers piping, at least in England.
- Eleven Ladies Dancing: The dancing of course is a code word for passion and courtship. The dancing

ladies are Lapwings that wildly, wheel, roll and tumble in the air during courtship displays.
- Twelve Lords A-Leaping: The lords a-leaping are cuckoos. And the cuckoo hen notoriously lays her eggs in another bird's nest. Because of this the cuckoo became a symbol of immorality and disorder. Not just this day, but the whole season of twelve days was a time of misrule and sexual license. The world was turned upside down. During these twelve days, right is wrong, the strong are weak, the first is last, and the lowliest laborers might become the highest lords.

Arius: First Council of Nicaea

The First Council of Nicaea was a council of Christian bishops convened in Nicaea in Bithynia by the Roman emperor, Constantine I in 325 CE. This first Ecumenical council was one of the first efforts to attain consensus in the Church through an assembly; although previous councils, including the first Church, the Council of Jerusalem, had met before to settle matters of dispute.

Its main accomplishments were settlement of the Christological issue of the nature of Jesus and his relationship to God, the construction of the first part of the Creed of Nicaea, establishing uniform observance of an Easter, and promulgation of early canon law.

The First Council of Nicaea was the first ecumenical council of Christianity. Derived from Greek; "oikumene", ["the inhabited land"] ecumenical means "worldwide", but is generally assumed to be limited to the inhabited earth. [Danker (2000)]

One purpose of the council was to resolve disagreements arising from within the Church of Alexandria, over the nature of Jesus' relationship to God; in particular, whether Jesus had been begotten from his own being (i.e. eternally existing without a beginning) and therefore having no beginning, or else created out of nothing, and therefore having a beginning. [Kelly, (1978)] St. Alexander of

Alexandria and Athanasius took the first position; the popular presbyter, Arius; also from Alexandria, Egypt took the second view.

The council decided against Arius and his supporters overwhelmingly. Of the attendees, all but three (including Arius) agreed to sign the creed. These three were banished to Illyria. [Schaff & Schaff (1910)]

Another result of the council was an agreement on Easter. This was decreed in an Epistle to the Church of Alexandria which read: "We also send you the good news of the settlement concerning the holy Pasch, namely that in answer to your prayers this question also has been resolved. All the brethren in the East who have hitherto followed the Jewish practice will henceforth observe the custom of the Romans and of yourselves and of all of us who from ancient times have kept Easter together with you." [Seven Ecumenical Councils p.114]

The council was the first in which the technical aspects of Christology were discussed. [Kieckhefer (1989)]

Constantine invited 1800 bishops of the Christian Church (about 1,000 in the East and 800 in the West), but a smaller and unknown number not exceeding 318, attended. The Eastern bishops formed the great majority of those who attended.

After being in session for more than a month, the council promulgated on June 19 the original Nicene Creed. This profession of faith was adopted by all the bishops, except three, including Arius.

The Arian controversy arose in Alexandria when the newly re-instated presbyter Arius, conflicted with his bishop, St. Alexander of Alexandria over doctrinal views. The disagreement sprang from different ideas about the 'Godhead', and what it meant for Jesus to be 'God's son'.

Alexander maintained that the 'son' was divine in just the same sense that the 'father' is, and co-eternal with the 'father'. Arius on the other hand taught that the 'son' had a beginning, and that he possessed neither the eternity nor the divinity of 'the father'. That the 'son' was rather the very first and the most perfect of God's creatures. [Davis. Leo Donald (1983), The First Seven Ecumenical Councils 325-787]

According to some accounts, the debates became so heated that at one point Arius was struck in the face by Nicholas of Myra, who would later be canonized.

Much of the debate hinged, on being born or created, and being begotten. According to surviving accounts, Arius argued for the supremacy of God and maintained that Jesus was created as an act of God's will – and therefore that he was a creature made by God. [Cyclopedia of Biblical, Theological and Ecclesiastical Literature]

Arians cited the verse which mentions Jesus as the firstborn off all creation in Colossians 1: 15 as evidence for their argument.

The council at its close declared that Jesus was god, co-eternal with 'the father'. This belief was expressed by the bishops in the creed of Nicaea. From the Council of Nicaea, one specific creed was used to define the Church's faith clearly, to include those who professed it and exclude those who did not.

The works of Arius were ordered to be confiscated and consigned to the flames, while any persons found possessing them were to be executed. [Schaff (1910)]

The suppression of the Meletian Schism was also discussed by the council. The Meletians were joined with Arius, causing more dissension than ever, being among the worst enemies of Athanasius. The Meletians ultimately died out around the middle of the fifth century.

Arius

Although all positive writings on Arius' theology have been suppressed or destroyed, negative writings describe Arius' theology as stating that there was a time before Jesus, when only God existed.

Reconstructing the life and doctrines of Arius has proven to be a difficult task, as none of his original writings survive. It is from the quotations available in the works of Church men who deemed him heretic, that we are able to know his teachings.

Arius was possibly of Libyan Berber descent. His father's name is given as Ammonius. Although his character has been severely assailed by his opponents, Arius appears to have been a man of personal ascetic achievement, pure morals and decided convictions.

Paraphrasing Epiphanius of Salamis, an opponent of Arius, Catholic historian, Warren H Carrol describes him as tall and lean, of distinguished appearance and polished address. Women doted on him, charmed by his beautiful manners, touched by his appearance of ascetism. Men were impressed by his aura of intellectual superiority. [Carrol. A, History of Christendom, Vol. 2]

The accusation of Arius' his opponents that he was too liberal, and too loose in theology, engaging in heresy, has been refuted by historians who argue that he was actually quite conservative, and that he deplored how, in his view, Christian theology was being too freely mixed with Greek Paganism. [Williams. Rowan (2002) Arius (Revised ed.)

Arius is notable primarily because of his role in the Arian controversy, a great 4th century theological conflict that rocked the Christian world, and led to the calling of the first ecumenical council. [Hanson. R P C (2007) The Search for the Christian Doctrine of God]

The Trinitarian historian, Socrates of Constantinople reports that Arius sparked the controversy that bears his name when St. Alexander of Alexandria gave a sermon stating the similarity of Jesus to God. Arius interpreted Alexander's speech as being a revival of "Sabellianism", condemned and argued against it.

Sabellianism in the Eastern Church, or Patripassianism in the Western Church is the belief that God, 'the son' and Holy Spirit are three different modes or aspects of one monadic God, rather than three distinct persons within the 'God-head'. [Stokes. G T, Sabellianism ed]

The Bishop of Alexandria exiled Arius for this. Arius' supporters vehemently protested. Arius is said to have enjoyed the support of numerous bishops for his cause. Among his supporters was Eusebius of Nicomedia. [Rubinstein. Richard, When Jesus Became God: The Struggle to Define Christianity during the Last Days of Rome]

"Thus said Arius, God's first thought was the creation of 'the son', before all ages, therefore time started with the creation of the Logos or Word in Heaven" [Arius Thalia, Fourth Century Christianity]

Constantine I

Constantine I was a Roman emperor from 306 to 337 CE. He is considered to be the first Christian emperor who called the First Council of Nicaea in 325 CE.

Beginning with the Renaissance, there were critical appraisals of his reign due to the rediscovery of anti-Contantinian sources. Critics portrayed him as a tyrant.

Constantine ordered the construction of the Church of the Holy Sepulchre (supposed tomb of Jesus) in Jerusalem, which became the holiest place in Christendom. The Papal claim to temporal power is based on the "Donation of Constantine". Constantine was given sainthood by the Anglicans, Byzantine Catholics and Eastern Orthodox Christians.

He appears to have usurped power – judging from how he became emperor.

Following the First Council of Nicaea, he enforced the prohibition against celebrating the Lord's Supper on the day before the Jewish Passover (14 Nisan). This marked a definite break from the Judaic tradition. From then on, the Roman Julian calendar, a solar calendar, was given precedence over the luni-solar Hebrew Calendar, among the Christian Churches.

Early Followers of Jesus

"Ebionites" is the term used for referring to the Jewish Christian movement that existed during the early centuries of Christianity. They regarded Jesus as the Messiah, while rejecting his divinity. [Ebionites, Encyclopedia Britannica]

They insisted on the necessity to follow Jewish law and rites.

They used only one of the Jewish Gospels, revered James, the Just, and rejected Paul of Tarsus as an apostate from the Law. [Maccoby. Hyam (1987) The Mythmaker: Paul and the Invention of Christianity] Much of what is known about the Ebionites derives from the Church fathers, who wrote polemics against the Ebionites.

Origen wrote: "For Ebion signifies "poor" among the Jews, and those Jews who have received Jesus as Messiah are called by the name of Ebionites." [Origen, Contra Celsum, ii]

The "Carpocratians" were another of the groups of early Followers of Jesus. The earliest and most vivid account of the Carpocratians comes from Iranaeus (died; 202 CE), in his "Against Heresies".

They believe, he writes, that "Jesus was not divine; but because his soul was steadfast and pure he remembered those things which he had witnessed within the sphere of the un-begotten God."

Early Divisions between Paul of Tarsus and the Jerusalem Church (Peter and James)

Peter and James were at odds with the teachings of Paul (after whom, Pauline Christianity). "I opposed Peter to his face because he was wrong" – Paul [Galatians 2]

Paul went on to mention that the differences were not just with Peter but with James and the Jerusalem Council.

Among the things they disagreed over was circumcision, which Paul sought to exclude as a must for converting men and women. The Antioch Incident, which found Paul in violation of the Laws of the "Noahide" Covenant against Idolatry, is another evidence of Paul's straying from the beliefs and practices of the Jerusalem Church. Paul was sternly rebuked and made to answer charges in Acts 21, concerning his violation of the Torah and misrepresentation of Yeshua's (Jesus) teachings.

Following Paul's confrontation with Peter, there seemed to be no further contact between the two men and they ceased to have amicable relations. [S G F Brandon, The Fall of Jerusalem]

Barnabas also deserted Paul in the dispute - something that speaks volumes, since they were bosom buddies. The scandal is slurred over in Acts which tried to show Paul was always on good terms with the original disciples.

There were significant differences between Peter and Paul. The former was a born Jew who grew up in Galilee, knew Jesus personally, and was directly familiar with his precepts.

Paul was born in a prosperous, Gentile, urban center which served as the capital of the Roman province. He was raised in an environment where Paganism was ubiquitous and predominant. He never knew Jesus in his life. He claimed to have met Jesus in a vision.

In fact Paul never developed a kinship with the men who had been close to Jesus, such as his brother, James or his disciples who were the leaders of the Jerusalem council. He remained aloof from the people associated with Jesus, and his teachings. His religious ideas were contrary to those of Jesus' original followers.

He became the first of those who corrupted the place and teachings of Jesus. His teachings served as support for Pauline Christianity and its novel Trinitarian doctrine which were unshared by the original followers of Jesus and men, like Arius, facilitating another **human** havoc.

Original Incarnation: Philosopher's Stone & Rosicrucianism

It is difficult or even impossible to find literary resources detailing one comprehensive process of incarnation. Naturally, human beings would not want this to become common knowledge. At length, the only hope would be to become initiated into the mysteries of one of the prominent cults, but obviously such knowledge would be reserved for 'humans'.

Most of what I have been able to gather was made possible by divine clues in 2010. One of these, 'the meteorite Stone (mentioned in the cult of Cybele and Attis) helped me in keeping trace and ultimately piecing together this treatise.

Apart from the little information found in narratives about the cult of Cybele and Attis and the Dionysiac Mysteries, I have of use, the revelations about gene and DNA and the rest in resources on Rosicrucianism – a name I first came across in 2010.

The secret teachings of the Rosicrucians, such as their formulas and methods of spiritual transmutation are not revealed public by any author.

The alchemy of the Rosicrucians was mental and spiritual alchemy. Their literature is full of references to a Philosopher's Stone. It talks about an Elemental substance, tenuous in form – regarded as the most subtle form of matter known to Science. This elemental substance lies far back of the planes of electrons and ions, in the corpuscles – of which matter as commonly known is composed. It is this Elemental Substance (corpuscles) that is regarded as the Philosopher's stone.

What is the purpose or use of the Philosopher's Stone? The Philosopher's Stone is the facility which contains all the lives/Spirits of the Jinn when they are not incarnate. The Philosopher's Stone holds the spirits of the Jinns for 12 days, and releases that spirit into a fetus on the 13th day, to be reborn as a human being, or in the absence of a human fetus; into a modified animal like 'the dog'.

Jane Ellen Harrison notes this "splintering of a god/goddess ("Jinn") from a primary entity, assuming aspects of the original in the process". [Harrison. J E, (1992) Prolegomena]

Alchemy Circle

The Rosicrucian symbol of the cross surmounted by the Rose according to Rosicrucians indicates that the rose can be attained only by the suffering of mortal life. One part of the spirit/life of the Jinn is extracted and split in two. One part is left in the still living Jinn. The "Two-finger" sign now ubiquitous in our world signifies these two spirits of each Jinn born in our world. This art would have been learnt by Zeus/Odin, who hung on a **windy** tree for nine days whilst transfixed with a spear to his side.

Hand of "Sabazius"

Rock of Ages (Hymn)

Rock of Ages cleft for me

Let me hide myself in thee

Let the water and the blood

From thy riven side which flowed

Be of sin the double cure

Save me from its guilt and power

Not the labor of my hands

Can fulfill thy Law's demands;

Could my zeal no respite know,

Could my tears forever flow

All could never sin erase

Thou must save and save by grace

Nothing in my hands I bring

Simply to thy cross I cling;

Naked come to thee for dress

Helpless look to thee for grace:

Foul, I to the fountain fly,

Wash me savior, or I die

While I draw this fleeting breath

When mine eyes shall close in death,

When I soar to worlds unknown,

See thee on thy judgment throne

Rock of Ages, cleft for me

Let me hide myself in thee

The Rosicrucian works state: "Life is the essence of spirit". In other words, the spirit is the life in us.

So, we have the birth of Dionysos, part-man and part-jinn who starts the incarnation of Jinns as humans into our world. He reproduces, bringing other Jinns as humans into our world.

By Odin's sacrifice, Jinns were able to incarnate as humans. When they die, their spirit returns to the Stone which serves as a holding facility – from whence they are reborn.

Rosicrucianism

Rosicrucianism holds a doctrine or theology "built on esoteric truths of the ancient past which **concealed from the**

average man; provide insight into nature, the physical universe and the spiritual realm".

Rosicrucians are said to be great adepts who have already advanced far beyond the cycle of rebirth. Their mission was to prepare the whole world toward the coming "Age of Aquarius", which commenced in the 21st century.

According to Masonic writers, the Order of the Rose Cross is expounded in a major Christian literary work that molded the subsequent views of the western civilization; "The Divine Comedy" (1308-1321) by Dante Alighieri [Pike. Albert, (1872) Morals and Dogma of the Ancient and Accepted Scottish Rite of Freemasonry, XXX: Knight Kadosh]

According to the Anthroposophy founder, Rudolf Steiner, the mystery of the foundation of the Rosicrucian order in the early 14th centuries, relates to the birth of Christian Rosenkreuz in the 13th century and, his rebirth in the 14th century.

Figure 4. Symbol of the Phallic Cross.

The symbol of the Rose Cross represented in the oldest monuments as the "crux ansata" or ankh (a Tau cross with a ring or circle over it).

To the Rosicrucians, it is the symbol of life; of that life that emanated from the deity. The cross and rose together are therefore hieroglyphically to be read as the Dawn of Eternal Life which all nations have hoped for by the advent of a redeemer…a redeemer or messiah yet to come, if he has not already appeared. [Pike. Albert, Morals and dogma of the Ancient and Accepted Scottish Rites of Freemasonry]

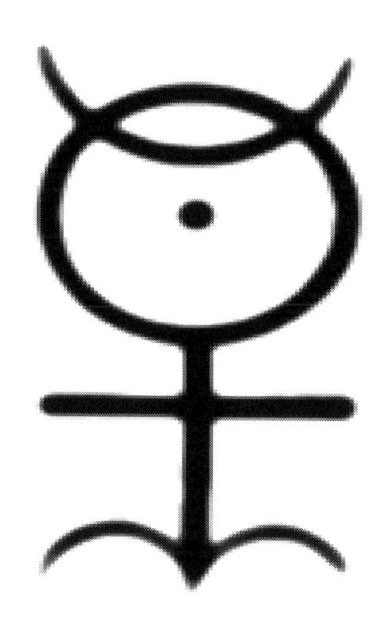

Dee's Hieroglyph

Central to the teachings of the Rosicrucians is the Philosopher's Stone. Terrence McKenna viewed the Philosopher's Stone as a "hyper dimensional union of spirit and matter" [Gyus' The End of the River: A critical view of Linear Apocalyptic Thought; and how linearity makes a sneak appearance in Time wave theory]

The legendary first manifesto, "Fama Fraternitas Rosae Crucis" (1614) inspired the works of Michael Maier. Maier made the firm statement that the Brothers of RC actually exist to advance the inspired arts and sciences. Maier was one of the most prominent defenders of the Rosicrucians, transmitting details in his writings. These writings point toward a symbolic and spiritual alchemy, rather than an operative one.

It was also the ideas of the Rosicrucians, embodied in a network of astronomers, professors, mathematicians and natural philosophers that gave rise to the Invisible College, the precursor to the Royal Society.

The general symbol of the order was a rose placed on the center of a cross.

For many years, little or nothing was permitted to be revealed to the general public, concerning the secret doctrine of the Rosicrucians, but during the past twenty-five years there has been a greater, and still greater freedom in this respect.

The little that was written or printed, concerning its body of teachings was disguised in the vague terms of alchemy and astrology, so that the same would have one meaning to the average reader and another closer meaning to those who possessed the key to the mystery. The frequent in the ancient books, to "sulphur", "mercury" and other chemical elements, and to the Philosopher's Stone were all intended to indicate certain portions of the teachings of the secret doctrine to those who already possessed the key.

The secret doctrine of the Rosicrucians is believed by those best informed to have been built up gradually, carefully and slowly by the old occult masters and Adepts, from the scattered fragments of the esoteric teachings which were treasured by the wise men of all races.

Magus Incognito, with respect to the absence of details on the Spiritual Transmutation, stated: "Such information cannot be cast broadcast, for reasons which will be apparent to every earnest and intelligent student… When the student learns how to give "the Right Knock", then will he find proven the old promise: "Knock and it will be given to you".

The well known symbol of the Rosicrucians, - "The Rosy Cross" – appears in several forms, as for instance: The cross surmounted by the rose, the sword (the cross handle) attached to the rose, and the cross surmounted by the crown; a modification of the Phallic cross.

The explanation of the general symbol is sevenfold – the three highest being reserved for initiates of the highest rank only.

1) The cross surmounted by the rose indicates that the rose can be attained only by the suffering of mortal life (symbolized by the cross)
2) The sword attached to the rose indicates that the sword of the spirit must be actively employed in the battle of life, in order to win the reward of the rose
3) The cross surmounted by the crown indicates that the suffering of mortal existence, borne by the faithful disciple of truth, will inevitably be rewarded by the crown of mastery. "Every cross (mortal life) has its crown; and no cross, no crown.

The Rosicrucian is directed to apply his attention to the concept of the world soul – the first manifestation of the parent.

The world soul is indicated by the dot in the circle in the hieroglyph. The circle represents the Infinite un-manifest, and the black dot represents the focal point of the new manifestation – the germ within the cosmic Egg.

An ever invisible bird dropped an egg into Chaos. Hence, "Brahm" was called "Kalahansa", the swan of eternity which laid at the beginning of each "Mahamanvantara", a golden egg. With the Greeks, this egg was part of the Dionysiac Mysteries, during which the egg was consecrated and its significance explained. The Christians – especially the Greek and Latin Churches, have fully adopted this symbol, and seen in it a commemoration of life eternal, or salvation and resurrection, found and corroborated by the custom of the Easter Egg.

Plane of the Elements

Here occurs the play between the atoms, the ions, corpuscles etc.

Plane of the Humans

At one pole, this plane is linked with, and blends into the sub-planes of the animal. At its other pole, it blends into the lower sub-planes of the next highest plane, the plane of the demi-gods.

According to the Rosicrucians, the animal lives its life and is contented, for it knows no better. If it has enough to eat, a place to sleep, a mate, it is satisfied and asks no more. They see many men as occupying little above this stage.

"As man progresses in the scale of Self-Consciousness, however he finds himself gradually detaching his sense of the Self from its sheaths and working tools. He begins to realize that there is an "I Am" within his being, to which all the feelings, the emotions, the desires and even the thoughts and ideas are but incidents".

"Even without calling upon the two still higher planes of consciousness, the enlightened race may reach heights of mental achievement which are so far above the average person" [The Secret Doctrine of the Rosicrucians by Magus Incognito]

The Souls' Progress

The Rosicrucians teach that the evolution of man is not confined to this planet, the earth, but rather is extended to a chain of seven planets.

These connected planets constituted the chain of worlds which is the series of homes of the individual soul, and the circuit of which is travelled by all individual souls. Not only does each individual soul now on earth reincarnate a number of times on this planet – but in the cause of the ages, will progress to the next highest planet.

Thou Hidden Source of Calm Repose (Hymn by Charles Wesley)

…I hide me Jesus in thy name…

In bonds my perfect liberty…

My life in death, my heaven in hell

Arise, My Soul, Arise by Charles Wesley

… His blood atoned for all our race

His blood atoned for all our race…

Five bleeding wounds he bears;

Forgive him, O forgive, they cry

Forgive him, O forgive, they cry

Nor let that ransomed sinner die!

Song by Donnie McClurkin

I am under the rock

The rock is higher than I

Jehovah hides me, hides me under the rock

Go tell my enemies that I am under the rock

Jehovah hides me, hides me under the rock

Nature of the Incarnates

"Primeval, two-natured, thrice-born, Bacchic lord, savage, ineffable, secretive, two-horned and two-shaped". [Orphic hymn about Dionysos, progenitor of the Incarnates]

Apart from the physical description already noted, all humans suffer from a hardly noticeable physical defect in their right eye. Odin's eye sacrifice affects every one of the Incarnates since he is their progenitor. On any close observance of their right eye, you will discover this defect. The "Al Seeing-Eye" stems from this. Odin is able to see through the eyes of each individual human on earth.

Humans enjoy stronger teeth that may be more resistant to cavities since they are created to exist for longer years – especially when compared to the lives of men. The heavy consumption of sweets and sweetened snacks would do less damage to their teeth.

Humans make very good sportsmen. They are particularly capable at football and basketball, cricket, baseball and hockey. Men make very good American footballers. The nature of the game suits our physicality very well, except for kicking the ball.

They may also be prevalent in the sciences. This may be fraudulent, since the method of enquiry and research which explain how men unravel the mysteries which are converted to our benefit may not be exactly responsible for the discoveries. Socrates' claim that knowledge is attained by recollection is one support for this.

The Incarnates greatly populate the coercive apparatus of the state. Other characteristics shared by them include sexual perversion. Promiscuity is a common lifestyle of the Incarnates. Men are not promiscuous in nature, and hardly ever cheat on their spouses.

Another thing which I put forward earlier is the incarnation of a female spirit into a male body and male spirit into a female body, which happens when a matching sex is not available. This, I propose, is the chief reason for homosexuality in today's world.

The male spirit in the female body remains attracted to a female. Hence, he seeks a female companion. The female spirit in the body of a male is attracted to a male, and therefore seeks a male companion.

"The Mona Lisa"

The Mona Lisa is perhaps the world's most well known painting. No other painting has been viewed more than the Mona Lisa. Leonardo da Vinci, who is the portrait's painter, is known for making observational drawings of anatomy and nature.

The Mona Lisa is the painting of a female form that is most likely of male essence (spirit).

The reason for its worldwide popularity and fame is most likely because it is a portrait of an incarnation of Zeus in female body.

Marcel Duchamp, one of the most influential modern artists created L.H.O.O.Q, a Mona Lisa parody, made by adorning a cheap reproduction with a moustache and a goatee. Duchamp added the description; "Elle a chaud au cul" [meaning; "she has a hot ass"]

There are many parodies of the Mona Lisa that you can look up. It is the most parodied painting of all time.

Another thing to note about male spirits that incarnate as females is that they commonly have big buttocks.

Have you struggled to understand paintings or to comprehend the complexities in interpretative arts? The reason is because these arts contain and express their history.

The chance for men to make thriving, successful careers out of painting is as a result very slim. The mind-boggling sums paid for ordinary looking pieces of art may have been incomprehensible to you. Well the source of the value of these pieces of art should now be known to you.

Humans are prone to diseases – especially strange diseases. Diseases were not a prominent part of our world prior to the incarnation of the Jinns. The professional practice of medicine would likely not exceed 2297 BCE.

Disease has been used to grow doubts in the hearts of men about God – out of the pity and sympathy Men feel for those afflicted by diseases.

Humans are often immodest and unruly. They may struggle with obeying laws and are often criminal. Crime and criminality are not common to men. The lifestyle of the Jinn in Elysium is different from the lifestyle of Men. The environment, resources and climate of Elysium suits the basic nature of the Jinn and ensures that he does not have to apply much work or effort for his living. The Jinn does not farm or build things with the application of physical effort. He is born with 'magical' abilities, which he uses to establish his home and basic physical structures.

Therefore, as a human, he is naturally 'revulsive' of the demands of reaping his livelihood – even though he is well physically capable.

The human differs in character from men. His behavior is influenced by what he knows of himself.

Humans are more at ease with reptiles like the snake whilst men are averse to snakes. They are the practitioners of magic, sorcerers and "marabouts" among Muslims. It is not in men's nature to conceive or practice magic.

The presence of humans in the communities; schools and colleges, and the bullying of young men is in my view the reason why young men in utmost irritation, suppression and despair have wrongly taken their lives and the lives of others – to the point that the US State of Texas is now considering allowing students to carry arms on campus, for self-defense.

It may be noteworthy that these massacres are carried out by males – not females.

Having gone through school, you will agree with me on the bullying often perpetrated at school; the in-group male/female associations that contrive – convene to make life undesirable for some. Girls do not undergo this tortuous experience. It is as a result of this that young men, feeling battered and torn of the smallest ego decide to end the lives of others as well as theirs.

With advantage of knowing each other (as humans) and being able to commune together socially, they organize to achieve various purposes.

You may have found yourself in these situations; situations were some come together to and agree – to your exclusion, your loss in arguments or your failure to get people to agree with you (even when you are right).

Humans are mostly impatient. They also tend to love and become addicted to narcotics. Men tend to experiment with cannabis but do not last for a long time as cannabis smokers.

The Incarnates tend to age quickly and poorly. They may suffer wrinkled skin at an earlier age or become slightly physically deformed as they age.

As noted, they make up most of the world's sportsmen, enjoying more agility and endurance. They celebrate this agility every four years in the world games. Men are fast runners but do not enjoy the endurance common with those who run marathons.

For those of you disgusted (like me) with the Matadors and Bull runners, you now know where this originates and would see that men have no need in practicing such barbaric sports. It can be traced to the spearing of the bull in the Taurobolium sacrifice as part of the mysteries of Greece, and later, Rome.

Finally, humans are those with triple-stranded DNA and those with Rhesus negative genes who form 15% of world population. Be sure that it is they who occupy the offices of power and control the wealth of the earth.

The Jinns from the tribe of Zeus number some 333 million. These 333 million split from their spirit two parts which became incarnated in our world. They were joined by another 167 million from the other two, tribes. Since each one is two, these 500 million are incarnated as one billion humans on earth.

Ancient Egypt, Cleopatra and the Egyptian Tragedy

Akhenaten is the pharaoh who ruled Egypt in the time of Moses, and of whom much is related in the Qur'an. He was an idolater and tyrant, who was ruthless to those who contested his policies. He went as far as declaring himself to be God.

Akhenaten (living spirit of "Aten") was known before the fifth year of his reign as Amenhotep (meaning; Amun is satisfied). He ruled for seventeen years, and died perhaps in 1336 or 1334 BCE. He is especially noted for abandoning traditional Egyptian religion and introducing worship centered on the "Aten". He was called "the enemy" or "that criminal" in archival records.

He was all but lost from history, until the discovery during the 19th century of the city of Amarna, which he built for the "Aten".

Amenhotep IV was crowned in Thebes, and there he started a building program. He decreed the construction of a temple dedicated to the "Aten" in Eastern Karnak.

He embarked on the wide scale erasure of traditional 'gods' names, especially those of Amun.

Much of the art and building infrastructure created during Akhenaten's reign was defaced or destroyed in the period following his death. It has been proposed that he may have taken some of his daughters as sexual consorts.

Letter to the Pharaoh, Akhenaten from one of his commanders:

"To the king, my lord, my god, my sun, the sun from the sky; Message from Yapahu, the ruler of Gazru, your servant, the dirt at your feet. I indeed prostrate myself at the feet of the king, my lord, my god, my sun…seven times and seven times on the stomach and on the back. I am indeed guarding the place of the king, my lord, the sun of the sky, where I am, and all the things the king, my lord, has written me, I am indeed carrying out everything. Who am I, a dog. And what is my house…and what is anything I have, that the orders of the king, my lord, the sun from the sky, should not obey constantly?" [Moran (2003)]

Initially, Akhenaten presented Aten as a variant of the familiar supreme deity, Amun. However, by year nine of his reign, Akhenaten declared that Aten was the supreme and only God, and that he, Akhenaten was the only intermediary between Aten and the people.

Large scale corruption defined Akhenaten's reign that was unprecedented in Egypt. This was a problem that the last 19th century dynasty Pharaoh, Horemheb, was compelled to deal with – even threatening to cut off the nose of any officials who were found to be involved in state corruption or abuses.

Some see Akhenaten as a practitioner of an Aten monolatry. He refrained from worshipping any but Aten, while expecting the people to worship, not Aten, but him.

Tutankhamun was an Egyptian pharaoh (1332-1323 BCE). His name means "image of Amun".

In his third regnal year, Tutankhamun reversed several changes made during Akhenaten's reign. He ended the worship of the god, Aten and restored the worship of Amun to supremacy in Egypt, restoring traditional priviledges to the religion.

"Amun"

Amun, (also; Amen) was a major Egyptian and Berber deity. He was the transcendental, creator deity. Amun was the champion of the poor or troubled and central to personal piety. [Tobin. Vincent Arieh, Oxford Guide: The Essential Guide to Egyptian Mythology] His position as the King of gods developed to the point of virtual monotheism, where other gods became manifestations of Him.

The name Amun meant something like the hidden One or Invisible. [Hart. George, (2005) The Routledge Dictionary of Egyptian gods and goddesses]

As already noted, amun is the one God of the Abrahimic faiths. Apart from this identity as the Creator God, which still survives, resources proving this assertion are scant or largely unavailable.

Cleopatra VII

Cleopatra VII reigned as Pharaoh of Egypt between 51-12 BCE. She is the Pharaoh who conspired with Julius Caesar to dethrone her co-rulers, Ptolemy XIII and Arsinoe IV, and rule Egypt as sole ruler.

The name "Cleopatra" means "she who comes from glorious father".

In 51 BCE, relations between Cleopatra and her consort, Ptolemy XIII completely broke down after Cleopatra dropped Ptolemy's name from official documents, and her face alone appeared on coins. This went against Ptolemaic traditions of females being subordinate to male rulers.

Cleopatra tried to raise a rebellion around Pelusium, but was soon forced to flee. [Green. Peter, (1990) Alexander to Actium: The Historical Evolution of the Hellenistic Age]

When Caesar (Julius) was in Egypt, Cleopatra had herself secretly smuggled in Caesar's palace to meet with him. She was smuggled past Ptolemy's guards, rolled up in a carpet. She became Caesar's mistress, and nine months after their first meeting, in 47 BCE gave birth to their son, Ptolemy Caesar. Caesar would help Cleopatra become sole ruler of Egypt.

Caesar erected a golden statue of Cleopatra in Rome, in the temple of Venus Genetrix, situated at the Forum Julium.

The Roman orator, Cicero said in his preserved letters that he hated the foreign queen. [Cicero, Letters to Atticus] She called herself Nea Isis. Egyptians believed that she was the reincarnation of the goddess Isis (Cybele).

Cleopatra is reported by some to have been of great beauty. Plutarch though, casts doubt on this, and says that: "Her beauty as we are told, was in itself neither altogether incomparable, nor such as to strike those who saw her". [The Beauty of Cleopatra. University of Chicago]

After Mithridates raised the siege of Alexandria, Caesar defeated Ptolemy's army at the Battle of the Nile. Before this, the warring factions fought in mid December 48 BCE. They fought inside Alexandria, which suffered serious damage, including the burning of some of its buildings, which comprised the Library of Alexandria. Caesar only triumphed when reinforcements arrived. According to some sources he was nearly killed.

Cleopatra VII [Altes Museum, Berlin]

Upon his victory, he took Arsinoe IV captive, transporting her to Rome, where in 46 BCE she was forced to appear in Caesar's triumph.

She was granted sanctuary at the temple of Artemis, where according to some reports, she was in 41 BCE, on the steps of the temple on orders of Mark Anthony, who some say was instigated by Cleopatra.

In the 1990s, an octagonal monument situated in the center of Ephesus was proposed by Hilke Thur of the Austrian Academy of Sciences to be the tomb of Arsinoe IV.

Hilke Thur examined the old notes and photographs of the now missing skull and concluded that it shows signs of an admixture of African and Egyptian ancestry. [BBC One Documentary, Cleopatra: Portrait of a Killer]

Cleopatra herself was a Mulatto of mixed Greek and Egyptian ancestry.

Cleopatra's subversion and the consequent Roman ruler ship of Egypt put an end to the African dynasty and rulers which had ruled Egypt. Ptolemy XIII was the last of Egypt's African rulers and the last pharaoh who worshipped Amun.

Cleopatra's ascension to the throne paved the way for much of the polytheism and paganism proper that would be rampant and ubiquitous in Egypt.

Arthur, Brittania and Marianne

King Arthur is a legendary British leader who, according to medieval histories led the defense of Britain against Saxon invaders in the late 5th and early 6th centuries CE.

Arthur is a central figure in the legends making up the so-called "Matter of Britain". Geoffrey of Monmouth's fanciful 12th century, "Historia Regum Britanniae" (History of the Kings of Britain), presents Arthur as a great warrior, a king of Britain who defeated the Saxons and established an empire over Britain, Iceland, Ireland, Norway and Gaul.

Arthurian literature thrived during the Middle ages, but waned in the centuries that followed, until it experienced a major resurgence in the 19th century. In the 21st century, the legend lives on, not only in literature but also in adaptations for theater, film, television, comics and other media.

Thomas Green identifies three key strands to the portrayal of Arthur. The first is that he was a peerless warrior who functioned as the monster hunting protector of Britain from all internal and external threats, such as the Saxons he fights in the Historia Brittonum, but the majority is supernatural, including giant cat-monsters, destructive boars, dragons, dog-heads, giants and witches.

The second is that Arthur was a figure of folklore and localized magical wonder- tales. The third and final strand is that the early Welsh Arthur had a close connection with the Welsh otherworld "Annwn". On the one hand, he launches assaults on otherworldly fortresses in search of treasure, and frees their prisoners. His war band in the earliest sources, include former pagan gods, and his wife and his possessions are clearly otherworldly in origin.

In the Idylls, Arthur became a symbol of ideal manhood, who ultimately failed to establish a perfect kingdom on earth.

In the latter half of the 20th century, the influence of the romance tradition of Arthur continued through novels such as T H White's, "The Once and Future King".

King Arthur was the incarnation of the son of Odin (Zeus), Thor or Ares. This personality is the appointed (false) messiah of Satan (Odin), whose return was awaited by some.

Britannia

Britannia may be the name for a confederation of Jinns (Gog & Magog). Britannia is depicted with an image of one of their matriarchs, Diana/ Artemis.

Rule Britannia (Song)

When Britain first, at Heaven's command arose from out azure main

Arose, arose from out the azure main

This was the charter, the charter of the land

And guardian angels sang this strain

Rule Britannia, Britannia rule the waves!

Britons never, never, never shall be slaves

Rule Britannia, Britannia rule the waves!

Britons never, never, never shall be slaves.

The nations not so blessed as thee,

Must in their turns to tyrants fall,

Must in their turn to tyrants fall,

While thou shalt flourish great and free

The dread and envy of them all

Rule Britannia, Britannia rule the waves!

Britons never, never, never shall be slaves

Rule Britannia, Britannia rule the waves!

Britons never, never, never shall be slaves.

Still more majestic shalt thou rise,

More dreadful from each foreign stroke;

More dreadful, dreadful, from each foreign stroke

As the loud blast, the blast that tears the skies

Serves but to root the native oak

Rule Britannia, Britannia rule the waves!

Britons never, never, never shall be slaves

Rule Britannia, Britannia rule the waves!

Britons never, never, never shall be slaves.

Thee haughty tyrants ne'er shall tame;

All their attempts to bend thee down

Will but arouse, arouse thy generous flame,

But work their woe, and their renown

Rule Britannia, Britannia rule the waves!

Britons never, never, never shall be slaves

Rule Britannia, Britannia rule the waves!

Britons never, never, never shall be slaves.

The muses still with freedom found

Shall to thy happy coast repair,

Shall to thy happy, happy coast repair

Blest isle with matchless, with matchless beauty crowned

And many hearts to guide the fair

Rule Britannia, Britannia rule the waves!

Britons never, never, never shall be slaves

Rule Britannia, Britannia rule the waves!

Britons never, never, never shall be slaves.

The waves mentioned in the song could not mean ocean waves. Rather, it is another kind of wave. There is a type of wave that is everywhere. This kind of wave has been described as a disturbance which travels through a medium, from one location to another.

To understand the nature of a wave, it is important to understand the medium as a collection of interacting particles. The interactions of one particle of the medium with the next adjacent particle allow the disturbance to travel through the medium.

A wave transports energy and not matter. When a wave is a present in a medium (that is when there is a disturbance moving through a medium), the individual particles of the medium are only temporarily displaced from their rest position. There is always a force acting upon the particles that restores them to their original position. Mechanical waves and electro-magnetic waves are two important ways that energy is transported in the world around us. Waves in water and sound in air are two examples of mechanical waves. Electro-magnetic waves differ from mechanical waves, in that they do not require a medium to propagate.

Electro-magnetic waves unlike mechanical waves can travel through the vacuum of space.

The Rays, the divine evolution of the peoples and planets are represented by seven colors (new age) and more five colors (new age, gold or solar rays).

The colors of new age and solar rays are in order:

1. Blue (Power of faith)
2. Yellow (Obedience)
3. Pink (Beauty; geniality)
4. White (Ascension; peace, light)
5. Green (Nature)
6. Red (True Resurrection)
7. Violet (New age of Master Saint Germain)
8. Turquoise (Lucidity)
9. Magenta (Divine wonder; Justiciars)
10. Gold (Materialization of wealth)
11. Orange (Sunshine)
12. Opaline (Renewal)

The waves in the Rule Britannia song may refer to more than just oceanic waves but instead, to the dominion of the universe. Rule Britannia is the unofficial anthem of the United Kingdom.

The Rays that I listed may explain the concept of the waves in the song. These twelve rays appear to include every facet of life.

It is clearly absurd that Britain would to date revel in the proffered maritime accomplishments which many cite to explain this song. Besides, mankind have plied and built ships for years. Britain's position in the world around the time when the song was released was much more than just naval supremacy and greatness.

Britannia is also used to refer to the Isles' goddess, Diana or Minerva. She is one of the two wives of Jupiter (Odin).

It was the Greco-Roman term for Great Britain and the female personification of the land as a goddess, armed with trident and shield and wearing a Corinthian helmet. She appeared on all the coins, until seven years ago (2008). Nowadays, she is just on the 2 pound coin. Britannia is to the United Kingdom what Marianne is to France, and what Columbia is to the United States.

Gilray cartoon on the 1803 "Peace of Amiens" features a fat

Britannia kissing "Citizen Francois"

Marianne

Marianne is a national symbol of the French Republic and a portrayal of the goddess of Liberty.

Marianne is displayed in many places in France and holds a place of honor in town halls and law courts. Her profile stands out on the official government logo of the country, is engraved on French Euro coins, and appears on French

Postage stamps. It was featured on the former Franc currency.

She is often portrayed with the Phyrgian cap. The seal of the state decreed in 1792 shows Marianne holding a spear, with a Phyrgian cap held aloft on top of it. Until 1792, the image of Marianne was overshadowed by other figures such as mercury and Minerva.

By 1793, the conservative figure of Marianne was replaced by a more violent image; that of a woman bare-breasted and fierce of visage.

Two 'Mariannes' were authorized. One is fighting, recalling the Greek goddess, Athena: she dons the Phyrgian cap and a red corsage, and has an arm lifted in a gesture of rebellion. The other is more conservative: she is rather quiet, wearing clothes in a style of Antiquity, with sun rays around her head, and is accompanied by many symbols; wheat, plough and the fasces of the Roman lictors.

Columbia

Columbia is a historical and poetic name used for the United States of America, and also as one of the names for its female personification.

The United Kingdom, France and the US are personified as pseudo-classical goddesses named with Latin names.

Unnamed by the Romans, 'Columbia' was the closest the Americans came to emulating this custom. The personification of Columbia was largely replaced by the Lady Liberty as a feminine allegory of the United States.

In the 19th century, Columbia was visualized as a goddess-like female national personification of the United States.

What we see here is the honoring and share of territories between the two wives of Zeus, namely; Diana/Libera (Britannia) and Hera/Ceres (Marianne).

To Diana, the United Kingdom or British territories like Canada and Australia while France and the United States are bequeathed to Hera.

Since by the incarnation process, it is difficult to be born in one's own territory again and again, these two are born into each other's territory. Privilege and position means they ascend the throne in each other's territory and assume the position of high office. One notable example may be Victoria, who ruled from 1837 to 1901. This personality was most likely Hera, incarnate. The above portrayal of her in status as Britannia is suggestive also of the accession/cooperation that Britain would have enjoyed from France, during her time.

A depiction of Columbia

My Story

In 2010, the realization set upon me – just how I had lived the lie and assumption that life in the west was great, affluent and fair for its masses. First, there was the banking default and the subsequent bailout of the banks. Then I watched as enforcement authorities came down heavy on peaceful protests. In one of these in England, an innocent passer-by was killed by the blows of a police officer.

When I first began to grasp the injustice of Treasury Bonds, I felt outrage within me – a bond business which simply makes the rich richer. It defeats my understanding to see states in the 21st century still being bailed out by the wealthy; states working for the satisfaction of the financial interests of those with outrageous amounts of finance, who buy government bonds and later sell them back with huge interests.

These same individuals own and run the banks that enjoy government rescue in the face of threatened collapse. For many, it was the more astounding when in the same period, the banks which had been bailed out with tax payers money returned to paying large bonuses to staff in the same period.

During my time in England, I worked as a Domestic and later, as Kitchen Porter at a canteen. I saw Catering/Cooking as one area of promise, and myself, as having potential to do well with the skill in a future enterprise back at home. The tortuously unbearable physical experience of working in the kitchen ensured that I quit after nearly three months.

My day began at 7:00 am when I would start with moving deliveries from the back entrance to the kitchen.

After packing the contents of some eight or more crates into the freezer room, refrigerator and store, I would proceed with readying the ovens and preparing plates and cutlery in the dining area. By the end of this, breakfast would have been served. Work then fully commences.

As the utensils for preparing breakfast, namely, trays, pots, and pans are used I quickly wash and make them ready for a second or third use. As the plates and cutlery are used by staff having breakfast, I retrieve them from the dining hall and make them ready for use again. This continues for about two hours.

Perhaps because of a shortage of staff, I am asked to help with the preparation of vegetables. This may include peeling a large, full bag of onions and half a bag of potatoes on a daily basis. At about 10:00, another delivery of ingredients and mostly beverages takes place. I would leave these Kitchen Assistant duties and sort this stock out. At the end of this I take a fifteen minutes break to have breakfast.

On my return from breakfast, the washing room would already be filled to almost the height of the ceiling with things to wash. I spend about an hour, thirty minutes reducing this pile and getting the dining hall plates and cutlery ready for lunch. With lunch served, I spend the hours between lunch and roughly 3:00 retrieving plates and cutlery from the dining hall and washing up both these and the ever streaming in kitchen utensils.

Between roughly 3:00 or 3:30 to 4:00 pm, I engage in taking out the trash and cleaning the kitchen. Intermittently, between days, I clean pack the freezer rooms and store. I return home knackered to start the day again at 5:00 am, as I had to make an hour, thirty minutes travel to work - five days a week.

By July 2010, I had lost all hope in whatever promise the west had for me. I felt like a slave, deep amidst the chasm of class and felt extremely poor for the first time in my life. There was nothing it appeared I could afford. I labored in sweat but I could not even afford to buy a lunch snack at times when I was hungry, returning home from a part-time job – after all the physical exertion. What was more annoying was the fact that the physical effort required to complete the work was clearly for me, vastly incommensurate to the remuneration I received.

By October, I had purchased an "Afriqiyah" Airways flight ticket to return home. October 2010 had found me once again practicing my faith to the fullest.

There was a time when I would have been conflicted by the social system in Islam. The economic injustices of the West were now more than apparent to me. Islam was fair and to me, no other system gave men more.

I spent a lot of time praying and embracing Islam, learning new chapters of the Qur'an, and pondering the dormancy of the Saudi leaders, who had the opportunity of changing the economic woes of the world, by the direct advocacy and propagation of what Islam advances on economy and welfare. I loathed the fact that they had established themselves as kings contrary to what is allowed in Islam. Kingship is for God.

In 2010, astronomers discovered the brightest star ever discovered – a colossal star known as R136a1, which is more than 265 times more massive than the sun, in the Tarantula Nebula region. It is millions of times brighter than the sun.

The discovery astonished scientists, who thought it was impossible for stars to exceed more than 150 times the mass of the sun. The R136a1 is in a cluster of stars known as RMC136a in a neighboring galaxy known as the Large Megallanic cloud.

There is a prophecy in Islam about the appearance of a star which would announce the approach of the Last Hour. This star is referred to in the 86th chapter of the Qur'an.

"By the heaven and the Knocker. And what can make you know what is the Knocker. It is the star of brightest star". [Qur'an 86: 1-3]

When this star's discovery was announced I took a strong note of it.

On 4th October 2010, the Ajka Alumina dam in Hungary collapsed. The dam collapsed releasing 700,000 cubic meters of alkaline red mud. The mud was released as 3-7 feet wave flooding several nearby localities, including the village of Kolontar and the town of Devescer.

About forty square kilometers of land was initially affected. The spill reached the Danube on 7th October, 2010.

The first thing I thought of was the dam Cyrus (Dhul Qarnain) built, which I had by now from research understood to be located in Eastern Europe. It's coming down would mean a phase had been reached in the life of Gog & Magog.

On the 14th October, something wonderful happened to me. At or about sunset, I stood, preparing to break my fast, when I began feeling the approach of someone from the northern sky. For two days, prior to the 14th I had suffered from extremely sharp pains in the lower right side of my abdomen. I had prayed about and resolved within me, not to worry – even though the pains were strong and fearful.

As I stood, my attention was drawn to the north sky. I could feel this entity approach with great speed and might, and his point of emergence seemed extremely far. With his coming everything the world seemed to have halted – but I knew that. It felt completely like only one was in motion at this time and everything else halted in recognition of him. Yet, I knew that activities would be ongoing in the world. It seemed like the earth was being reverend to this being. That day, time froze in my head.

I kept my sight fixed in the direction this being was coming from. Eventually, I could see that his approach was for my room. As I looked I managed to see the out-stretch of his wings as they dropped slowly, with his landing.

His wings would measure twelve feet from one end to the other. I did not see his face and the view of his exterior was exterior was faint. Within approximately two seconds of his landing, I felt something leave my anus – as if kicked out of me. I felt it clearly. I was to understand later that he kicked Satan who was trying to rupture my organs, out of me. Immediately, the pain stopped, and I would not feel it again. A new chapter had begun in my life.

The angel left, and in his place, the "Ruuh" (Holy Spirit), a being who was possibly Jesus, began communicating with me. He would leave me with teachings which would in time be the guide to understanding many things. I could hear him and he would know what I was thinking. He told me he wasn't within me.

I was left ill by the time he arrived. For seven nights, he flannelled off my body by means of some heat; expelling what may have been virulent matter from within me. For days after, I tried to put together materials for a book.

Online, he directed me to a picture of Prince Harry and told me he was the "Dajjal" (Anti-Christ). He directed me to a portion of Harry Potter and the Philosopher's Stone; the passage with the centaurs. He told me Centaurs did exist; at least at one time, and could read the stars correctly. He told me that the passage in the book was telling Satan and his cohorts that they were destined to fail. Ignoring this, they were insisting on against the reading of the centaurs.

The passage in Harry Potter and the Philosopher's Stone reads:

Bane: Have we not read what is to come in the movements of the planets?

Firenze: The planets have been read wrongly before now, even by the centaurs. I hope this is one of those times. – Harry Potter and the Philosopher's Stone [p.15]

At this point in 2010, the rebels still had days to end their opposition to "The God" and accept their place in life or be condemned to Hell – in the event their plan failed. I believe that only some thirty-eight million of those who incarnated made it.

Four thousand, three hundred and seven years after they began incarnating into our side of the world, the rebels had the chance of repenting and accepting the sovereignty of God over all. Yet they persisted and their deadline caught up with them.

On the 28th October, 2010, the Ten Nights that are the defining nights marking clear Man's place and the position of Jinns to Men began. The Ten Nights have been long awaited. These do not only confirm the correctness of God's making man superior to the jinn but it marked the consequent damnation of those who reject, blasphemed against God and rebelled, doing as they like. The Qur'an mentions the Ten Nights, but what it really stands for is not revealed. There exist different opinions regarding when the Ten Nights occur.

The Ten Nights are mentioned in chapter 89: 2 of the Qur'an in the chapter titled: "The Dawn".

"By the Dawn,

And by ten nights,

And by the even and the odd,

And by the night when it passes,

Is there not in all that an oath sufficient for one of perception?

[Quran 89: 1-5]

On the morning (dawn) of the 7th of November, 2010, I saw the Ruuh. He appeared to me while I was seated in a bus. He patted me on the right cheek with a kiss, and told me it was all over. I had gone through the first ten arduous nights of my life. Later, I understood what he said to mean Satan and his cohorts had failed, and victory had been attained by man. The Ten Nights were arduous for me but there was an even harder period I had to endure in England. On the 3rd of November, 2010, I ran into some trouble at Gatwick airport when I entered a restricted area. I had to appear before a Magistrate court as a result of this.

Upon the final hearing of my case, I was transferred on 7th December 2010 to the Immigration Removal Center since my visa had expired on the 3rd of November 2010.

I was to spend 77 days in the Immigration facility – during which, on the 18th of December, the Arab Spring began. These 77 days were so far the hardest days of my life. During the Ten Nights I had wished for death and regretted that I had ever known life. These 77 days were not to compare with them. I suffered like perhaps, no man had ever suffered before.

The behavior of those around me was strange. I recall talking to someone I assume was from Kenya, who asked me if I did not believe in "collective intelligence". I tried to tell him that God was too great and that if the entire world came together they would never be able to defeat God.

On the 25th of December, I was moved to a unit for eight people. I have forgotten the names of two of the people I shared the unit with, or what they were called. The names I remember are: Mohamed Saba, Gandalf, Alphonse, Husein, and one called "Preacher". The unit had two rooms and six beds. Strange things happened while I was in this unit, and it was during this time that I first began getting information about the Loa or Voodou spirits. I remember at one point the "Ruuh" telling me: "I gave them these things".

On the 2nd of January, I was moved to another unit. This facility seemed to confirm that I wasn't suffering from some illusion and gave credit to what I believed. On one occasion I was asked by someone who I had hardly met and who hadn't done me any wrong or hurt whatsoever, to forgive him. Strange also was two crying staff members.

Perhaps, the strangest incident was of a guy of Arab descent, who used his head to bang against the concrete wall, shouting: "We cannot win". Some days later, he came up to me with an apple and offered it to me. I accepted the apple. I returned to my home country on the 23rd February 2011.

I have come, since then, to believe that I was chosen to expose the enemy and the problems of our age. Since 2011, I have waited up to 2016 to receive again communication. The period we are now in appears to be a crucial one.

The rebellious Jinns and Gog & Magog are waiting to know the outcome of their efforts. It appears from one source that they have been told by their leaders that there is a 400 year delay from 2012, that they have to wait out – and not that hell now looms.

The news is that they failed, and Satan's respite is almost over. Victory has come and the word of God is fulfilled. All that remains is for men to retake their world and occupy the agencies of good action and prosperity.

The 110th chapter reads:

"When the help of God comes - and Victory! And you see men entering the religion of God triumphant. Then glorify with praises your Lord and seek His forgiveness. [Qur'an 110: 1-3]

I was shown in 2010 the verses of the 48th chapter and told that it was about our time.

"Certainly, We have given you victory; a victory manifest. That God may forgive you what preceded of your sin and what is to come after; and complete His favour upon you – and guide you to the straight path. And that God may aid you with a mighty victory". [Qur'an 48: 1-3]

I should include that during this time I was told that the world will end in this century. The duration of Men on earth would be 40,000 years from the time of Adam.

Anti-Christ and the Jews

The Tribe of Dan was one of the tribes of Israel. According to the Torah, the tribe consisted of descendants of Dan, a son of Jacob and Bilhah, Rachel's maidservant. [Genesis 30: 4]

Some have noted that the territory of the Handmaid tribes happens to be the closest to the north and eastern borders of Canaan, thus exposing them to Syria and Aram.

According to the Hebrew Bible, following the completion of the conquest of Canaan by the Israelite tribes, after about 1200 BCE, Joshua allocated the land among the tribes. Dan was said to be the last tribe to receive its territorial inheritance. [Petrie. George Laurens, (1910) Jacob's Sons]

The tribe was only able to camp in the hill country overlooking the Sorek Valley, the camp location becoming known as "Mahameh Dan" (Camps of Dan). [Joshua 19]

However, as a consequence of the pressure of the Philistines, the tribes abandoned hopes of settling near the center coast, instead migrating to the north of philistine territory, and after conquering Laish, re-founded it as their capital (renaming it Dan) [Judges 18]

In the Biblical census of the Book of Numbers, the tribe of Dan is portrayed as the second largest tribe after Judah. [Numbers 1: 39]

In Moses Blessing (Blessing of Moses) Dan is prophesied to leap from Bashan. Scholars are unclear why this should be, since the tribe did not live in the Bashan plain, east of the Jordan.

From after the conquest of the land by Joshua, until the foundation of the first Kingdom of Israel in 1050 BCE, the tribe of Dan was a loose confederation of Israelite tribes. No central government existed, and in times of crisis, the people were led by ad hoc leaders, known as Judges. The most celebrated Danite was Samson.

Samson, meaning; "man of the sun" [Dictionary of Deities and Demons in the Bible] is one of the last of the Judges of the ancient Israelites mentioned in the Hebrew Bible (Book of Judges).

Samson had two vulnerabilities; his attraction to untrustworthy women and his hair, without which he was powerless.

In licentiousness, he is compared with Amnon and Zimri. [Leviticus Rabbah. Xxiii. 9] Academics have interpreted Samson as a demi-god. [Leviton. Richard, (20140 The Mertowney Mountain Interviews] These views sometimes interpreted him as a solar deity, popularized by "solar hero" theorists and Biblical scholars alike. [Burney. Charles Fox, The Book of Judges with Introduction and Notes]

James King West finds that the hostilities between the Philistines and the Hebrews appear to be of a "purely personal and local sort". He also finds Samson stories to have an "almost total lack of moral and religious tone". [West. James King, (1971) Introduction to the Old Testament]

Dr Zvi Lederman, co-ordinator of the Tel Aviv University Beth Shemesh dig, believes that Beth Shemesh Canaanite village was a cultural meeting point on the border of the Israelite, Canaanite and Philistine areas and calls the stories border sagas, saying that Samson could cross boundaries, seeking a Philistine wife. Samson is said to have travelled to Gaza and stayed at a harlot's house. It is impossible to think that there would have been harlots among the Israelite community. Samson and those like him would have been left with this one option.

With the growth of the threat from Philistine incursions, the Israelite tribes decided to form a strong, centralized monarchy to meet the challenge, and the tribe of Dan joined the new kingdom, with Saul as the first king.

The oldest accounts of Saul's life and reign are found in the Hebrew Bible. He was reluctantly appointed by the prophet, Samuel, in response to a popular movement to establish a monarchy. He reigned from Gibeah.

After the death of Saul, all the tribes other than Judah, remained loyal to the house of Saul, but after the death of Ishbosheth, Saul's son and successor to the throne of Israel, the tribe of Dan joined the other Israelite tribes in making David, king of a reunited kingdom of Israel. However, on the accession of Rehoboam, David's grandson in 930 BCE, the northern tribes split from the house of David, to reform a kingdom of Israel as the Northern Kingdom.

Modern artists use the scales of Justice to represent the Tribe of Dan due to Genesis 49: 16 referencing: "Dan shall achieve justice for his kindred." However, traditional artists use a snake to represent Dan, based on Genesis 49:17. "Let Dan be a serpent by the roadside, a horned viper by the path that bites the horse's heel so that the rider tumbles backward".

Dan tribe plate Heichal Shlomo door, Jerusalem

Their primary trade characteristics was Sea-Faring; unusual for the Israelite tribes. [Mediterranean Archaeology, Vol. 16]

In the Song of Deborah, the tribe is said to have stayed on their ships with their belongings. [King. (1986) Cult and Calendar in Ancient Israel]

As part of the kingdom of Israel, the territory of Dan was conquered by the Assyrians, and they were exiled. The manner of their exile led to some of their history being lost.

According to the Book of Revelations 7: 4-8; along with the Ephraim, the tribe of Dan is one of the only original tribes of Israel that is not included in the list of tribes of Israel, which are sealed. It has been suggested that this could be because of their pagan practices. This made Hippolytus of Rome and a few Millenialists propose that the Anti-Christ will come from the Tribe of Dan.

You may by now have found something to be seriously wrong with the Israelite community. The weird habitation of boats or the Sea-faring occupation of the tribe of Dan would no less have been shocking to you. What you see, is an infiltration of the Israelite community by Gog & Magog, perhaps from their time in Egypt. It is this infiltration that would result in the stubbornness and disobedience to God's commands and the killing of prophets like Samuel and John (Yahya).

The foregoing should be enough for you to make out this infiltration. The house of Judah is the pure house of the Israelites. It is with the aid of this that this people have pioneered their Anti-Christ (false Messiah), corrupting the true Israelites and influencing the rejection of the true messiah when he came to our world.

Today, the tribe of Dan is in all likelihood the majority of the Jewish population. The Judaism promoted by these infiltrators is alien to the original religion.

It has gradually been assimilated with the Kabbalah beliefs which are totally alien to Abraham and Moses. These doctrines like what happened with other religions are mostly embraced by these infiltrators.

The true Children of Israel have probably been reduced to no more than 30% of the nation that claims descent from Yaqub (Israel), but with their help we can expose these impersonators. The strange practices now common among the Israelites would likely be questionable by them – but for the absence of some clue or knowledge pertaining to Gog & Magog, they would have not before now have been able to make out and identify these foreigners.

Contrary to what is now popular assumption, the Jews are not a hawkish seeking to establish global political and economic control. It is those who masquerade in their name that commit these horrors, leading to their being conceived by men like Hitler, as evil. Hitler, who was indeed wrong, and lacking in sufficient knowledge of this, reacted extremely, and in the process lost the economic prosperity he had introduced.

The men of the nation of Israel can now start enlightening us about their nation, their objectives and interests. This is important, and this is a calling to the man who is a descendant of Israel. It will help the world if he emerges and helps to establish these facts.

As noted, Hippolytus of Rome and other Millenialists proposed that the Anti-Christ will come from the tribe of Dan. This indicates that much was known about them around their time and also that they may have been notorious in the annals of that early history. It is in fact safe to assume that the paganism mentioned in the Bible would have been the handiwork of the tribe of Dan.

Identity of the Anti-Christ

The Anti-Christ, if we are to go by what has been reported is part Jewish. Today, some have discovered that Prince Harry's name when checked by a method involving Hebrew alphabet and numbers, gives a "666" equivalent. You may look this up on "youtube.com".

Prince Harry's mother is believed to be of Jewish ancestry. Certain sources maintain that the late Princess Diana's mother, Frances Shand Kyd was Jewish. She was born Frances Ruth Burke Roche; a Rothschild.

The Jews are the only nation among the Abrahimic faiths that have not accepted that the messiah has already come. They are the only ones still expecting the first coming of the messiah.

This has presented with opportunity, Satan, who with veiled moves institutes a system that appears to be the gradual unveiling of a world messiah. This is all for Satan to ascend, disguised, to an office of ruler ship of the world.

Renaissance, Science & Deception

The mysterious nature of the world and its complexities, which were once prevalent, have with the growth of science become well explainable. But these advances instead of serving to bolster our faith and the rationale for our belief in God, have in fact for the most of it been used (partly by direct attempts) to cause disbelief in Men.

The technology unearthed, which has made the production of goods and infrastructure possible, has made some men think themselves self-sufficient, with little faith in God. It is all the more exacerbated by the insufficient information in some religions, concerning the next life.

The technology and pleasures now available to us is not complemented by the short lifespan of men – the period of youth and post youth (up to 50) being too short for any of us to really enjoy life, amidst the pursuit of livelihood. I could not help but marvel at the infrastructure and lifestyle of the people in England, during my short stay in the country. With my background in religion and faith in God, I believe I was able to resist its power to overwhelm. I fear though that many men can be easily subsumed by its potency to distract one from God and the belief in an incomparable life ahead.

This last statement would quickly produce questions in your mind, as the only thing now apparently lacking is a life free from death and disease – or at least the realization of a much longer lifespan.

I would have had doubts that would have made me question whether really a life, incomparably greater than this awaits us in paradise. Those doubts (at least 99% of them) left me after I witnessed the mighty descent and appearance of an angel. Having already learnt much about God and the majesty of God, events in 2010 proved up to a 99% point the infiniteness of God to me.

The belief in God, much stressed by the 'trumpeters' of religion is not to enslave and transform you into easily controllable and manipulated individuals. Regrettably, the enemy, having infiltrated our society our society has made that so – thus making many steer clear of any God-conscious undertaking or lifestyle, especially also, due to the monastic forms of lifestyle – be it Muslim, Christian or Jewish.

Belief in God is a means to be reminded of Him, the self and the pitfalls that may make being successful difficult or unrealizable. Many things may ruin your life or suffer you to the point of failure. There are many traps in this world – traps that may lead to jail or suffering.

Science' awesome results could have been less captivating for men if they knew more about its origin, foundations and components. Science is not ordinary. I do not mean to say that it is dark, 'occultic' or evil. Science is from God. The application of it in nefarious ways is no doubt the fault of its practitioners.

I am sure that you, like me encountered the difficulties and perplexities of Mathematics, Physics or Chemistry, and struggled – after having cruised through Arithmetic. You may at the end have just decided it is not for you. There is nothing more hateful in school than having to go through those classes.

As for Mathematics, Physics and Chemistry, I really must wonder how we passed. Personally, it seems miraculous to me for a man to pass Chemistry or even to some extent, Physics.

The end result is often settling out of most of the self-employable professions. Just so I do not get harangued for making these points, I would at this juncture refer you to the Works of Plato and his dialogue on Arithmetic and Logistics.

Science is used today to delude and deceive men about the divine.

The revelations in the Qur'an, extraordinary as they are about the universe – which should have further established the faith of Men in the existence of God and the truth of the Messengers, like Muhammad for instance, have not been given due notice or acclaim. The various medium which glorify the achievements of Science deliberately refuse to bring to the fore these revealed facts. Mentioned in the Qur'an, is the verse: "And the heaven We constructed with strength, and indeed, We are its expander". [Qur'an 51:47]

This fact was discovered only in the 1970s by astronomers. The Qur'an mentions that the moon follows the earth as it orbits and also lists the embryonic stages of fetal development – revealing three trimesters.

These, if they had been given publicity and appropriate mention, would have probably affected men's faith positively.

The warning about Hell in the religions based on Monotheism is now taken on carelessly by some. Yet, the fact of the revelations regarding the universe and fetal development (now scientific knowledge), when coupled with the information revealed about the End times would have been enough for the pondering person to consider his/her life carefully.

I believe that the love of God is in every woman and man – a thing that blossoms with affection and longing.

Science has promoted the monkey origin theory which has made some men very much doubt in the divine. The evolving monkey it appears is in the course of its evolution becoming of increased ability – the academic notion that as he evolves he becomes increasingly able to accomplish many things.

Evolution theory has indisputably enjoyed much propagation and support. The theory itself is abhorrent to the child, compelled to learn about it in school. I, for one, found it abhorrent – even though I was not religious at age 11, 12 or 13. For this and other reasons I strove to disprove it.

The Evolution theory seems to define dark skinned people as the least evolved.

In light of the technology, now developed by humanity, and with most, if not all developed by light skinned people, it would appear from this, together if we consider the 'man becomes more able as he evolves theory', that the dark skinned man is still further behind in his evolution.

The color of man's eyes (some of which are not shared by dark skinned men) may be another indication that the dark skinned man is less evolved. Apart from this, even the hair we have may form part of another indication that the dark skinned man is least evolved.

In short, the closer similarity of features between the dark skinned man and the gorilla; like the flat nose, add to such suppositions – not forgetting that the dark skinned man lives closer to the gorilla, with the light skinned man (earlier evolved), having migrated to other parts long ago.

But there are questions that remain unanswered; like the birth of a Caucasian baby to dark skinned parents of African origin, in England, in 2010.

Another thing is the rapid, disparate growth of technology, which would indicate increased human ability over a relatively short, approximately 500 year period (1516 to date).

Man has lived on earth for at least 20,000 years. During at least 10,000 years he would have existed as Homo sapiens (sapiens). Now, how is it that he succeeded in inventing so little in say, a 9,500 year period while making extremely much more in say, a 1,000 to 500 year period?

Another question may be why aren't the animals evolving or taking on increased ability?

Away from earth, let us consider the other planets. Why is there no life on them? Or why has biological life not evolved on them?

Aside from Evolution, how is it that some massive galactic body has not collided with the earth?

Finally, the harmony of the earth, its perfect proportionate nature and sustained resourcefulness all indicate a design and is proof for us to believe in the existence of God.

The Science responsible for the technology and infrastructural development we now witness took proper form and undertaking in the 16th and 17th centuries, when an organized effort took root. This was called the Renaissance.

Renaissance

Renaissance is a period in Europe, from the 14th to 17th century, considered to be the bridge between the Middle ages and modern history.

The Renaissance's intellectual basis was its own invented version of humanism, derived from the rediscovery of classical Greek philosophy, such as that of Protagoras. In Science, it produced increased reliance on observation and induced reasoning.

The Fall of Constantinople generated a wave of émigré Greek scholars, bringing manuscripts.

In the first period of Italian Renaissance, humanists favored the study of humanities over natural philosophy or applied mathematics.

As the Protestant Reformation and Counter Reformation clashed, the Northern Renaissance showed a decisive shift in focus from Aristotelian natural philosophy to chemistry and the biological sciences (botany, anatomy and medicine).

Some have seen this as the acceleration of a continuous process stretching from the ancient world to the present day.

There is general argument that the Renaissance saw significant changes in the way the world was viewed and the methods sought to explain natural phenomena. [Brotton. J, (2006) Science and Philosophy: the Renaissance]

The important development was not any specific discovery, but rather, the further development of the process for discovery, 'the scientific method'.

It focused on empirical evidence, the importance of Mathematics, and discarded Aristotelian Science. Early and influential proponents of these ideas included Francis Bacon, Copernicus and Galileo.

The new scientific method led to great contributions in the fields of astronomy, physics, biology and anatomy.

Invisible College

Followers of Christian Rosenkreuz or the Rosicrucian order are believed to have started the Invisible College. The Invisible College is the pre-cursor to the Royal Society.

It was constituted by a group of natural philosophers who began to hold regular meetings to share and develop knowledge acquired by experimental investigation.

Among these was Robert Boyle, who wrote: "The cornerstones of the Invisible College (or as they term themselves, the Philosophical College) do now and then, honor me with their company". [Lomas. R, (2002), The Invisible College]

The concept of "Invisible College" is mentioned in German Rosicrucian pamphlets. Ben Johnson referenced the ideas related in meaning to Francis Bacon's "House of Solomon", in a masque, "The Fortunate Isles and their Union.

The term accrued currency for the exchange of correspondence within the "Republic of Letters".

Royal Society

The Royal started from groups of Physicians and natural Philosophers. They were influenced by the "new science" as promoted by Francis Bacon, in his "New Atlantis".

The society's motto: "Nallius in verba"; latin for, "Take nobody's word for it". It comes from Horace's Epistles, where he compares himself to a gladiator who, having retired is free from control.

Francis Bacon

Francis Bacon, Viscount Saint Alban, lord Chancellor of England, was a lawyer, statesman and philosopher.

He is remembered as a man who claimed all knowledge his province. After a magisterial survey urgently advocated new ways by which human beings might establish a legitimate command over nature for the relief of his estate, Bacon produced his "Instauratio Magna".

Francis Bacon's Instauratio Magna, eschewed the endless controversies in favor of a three-section structure, including external nature (the universe) covering such topics as astronomy, meteorology, geography and species of minerals, vegetables and animals.

Bacon's Instauratio Magna commenced a total reconstruction of sciences, arts, and all human knowledge, raised upon the proper foundations, in order to restore or cultivate a jest and familiarity between things and the mind. [Britannica Encyclopedia]

His approach to philosophy and nature is that there was much to discover about the laws of nature which it seemed to him needed much more exploration.

"But if there be any man who, not content to rest in and use the knowledge which has already been discovered, aspires to penetrate further; to overcome not an adversary in argument, but nature in action; to seek not pretty and probable conjectures but certain and demonstrable knowledge, with me, that passing by the outer courts of nature, which numbers have trodden, we may find a way at length into her inner chambers". [Novum Organum]

"Neither the naked hand, nor the understanding left to itself can affect much. It is by instruments and **helps** that the work is done, which are as much wanted for the understanding of the hand either give motion or guide it, so the instruments of the mind supply either suggestions for the understanding, or cautions". [Aphorism II]

Friedrich 'the great', Hitler

Friedrich II was King of Prussia from 1740 until 1786. He was nicknamed, Der alte Fritz ("Old Fritz") by the Prussian people.

In his youth, Friedrich was more interested in music and philosophy than the art of war. He defied his authoritarian father and sought to run away with his best friend, Hans Hermann von Katte. They were caught at the border and King Frederick William I nearly executed his son for desertion. After being pardoned, he was forced to watch the beheading of his friend, Hans.

Upon ascending to the Prussian throne, he attacked Austria and claimed Silesia during the Silesian Wars, winning in the process, military acclaim for himself and Prussia.

Near the end of his life, Frederick physically connected most of his realm by conquering Polish territories in the First Partition of Poland. He was an influential military theorist whose analysis emerged from his extensive personal battle field experience, and covered issues of strategy, tactics, mobility and logistics.

He was a proponent of Enlightened Absolutism and the first to modernize the Prussian bureaucracy and civil service.

Frederick II considered himself the first servant of the state. He reformed the judicial system and made it possible for men not of noble stock to become judges and senior bureaucrats. Frederick also encouraged immigrants of various nationalities and faiths to come to Prussia.

Nearly all 19th century German historians made Frederick into a romantic model of a glorified warrior, praising his leadership, administrative efficiency, devotion to duty and success in building up Prussia to a leading role in Europe. The Nazis glorified him as a great German leader.

Friedrich was brought up by Huguenot governesses and tutors, and learned French and German simultaneously. He was raised a Calvinist.

Friedrich was betrothed to Elizabeth Brunswick-Bevern a Protestant relative of the Austrian Habsburgs, but Friedrich himself proposed marrying Maria Theresa of Austria in return for renouncing the succession.

Frederick wrote to his sister: "There can be neither love nor friendship between us", and considered committing suicide. He went along with the wedding on 12th June 1738. Once Frederick secured the throne in 1740, he prevented Elizabeth from visiting his court in Potsdam, granting her instead Schonhausen palace and apartments at the Berliner Stadtschloss. Frederick would bestow the title of heir to the throne on his brother, since his wife begat him no children.

Before his accession, Frederick was told by D'Alembert: "The Philosophers and the men of letter in every land have long looked upon you, sire, as their leader and their model".

On his acquisition of Polish territories Frederick commented: "It is a very good and advantageous acquisition, both from a financial and a political point of view. In order to excite less jealousy, I tell everyone that on my travels I see just sand, pine trees, heath land and Jews. Despite that, there is a lot of work to be done; there is no order and no planning, and the towns are in a lamentable condition".

Friedrich transformed Prussia from a European backwater to an economically strong and politically reformed state. He protected the industries with high tariffs and minimal restrictions on domestic trade.

With the help of French experts he organized a system of indirect taxation, which provided the state with more revenue than direct taxation. He commissioned Johann Ernst Gotzkowsky to promote trade and to take on the competition with France - establishing a silk factory where soon 1,500 people found employment.

One of his greatest achievements included the control of grain prices, whereby government storehouses would enable the civilian population to survive in needy regions, where the harvest was poor.

Prussia's education system became one of the best during his reign. He modernized the Prussian bureaucracy and civil service, and promoted religious tolerance throughout his realm. He abolished most uses of judicial torture, except for the flogging of soldiers as punishment for desertion. "Prussian justice became the most prompt and efficient in Europe". [Langer. William, (1968) Western Civilization]

Friedrich aspired to be a Platonic philosopher king and stood close to the French Enlightenment. Friedrich though, disliked the German language and literature, explaining that German authors "pile parenthesis upon parenthesis, and often you find only at the end of an entire page the verb on which depends the meaning of the whole sentence".

He discarded many baroque era authors as uncreative pedants and especially despised German theater. He was unimpressed by the authors of the "Sturm und Drang" movement and remained of essentially classical taste.

Friedrich II was not appreciative of the luxury and extravagance of the French royal court, and he ridiculed German princes who indulged in those pleasures.

About a thousand new villages were founded during his reign that attracted 300,000 immigrants from outside Prussia. Using improved technology, enabled him to create new farmland through a massive drainage program in the country's Oderbruch marshland.

He presided over the construction of canals for bringing crops to market, and introduced new crops. He founded the first Veterinary School in Germany. Unusual for his time and his aristocratic background, he criticized hunting as cruel, rough and uneducated. Friedrich loved dogs and horses.

In 1752, he wrote to his sister that people indifferent to loyal animals would not be more grateful to other humans, and that it was better to be more sensitive than too harsh.

I have included this article on Friedrich 'the great' because I was told in 2010 that he was a man. His style of leadership should convince us of what is obtainable when a man is in power.

Adolf Hiedler

Adolf Hiedler (Hitler) was born an Austrian citizen and raised near Linz. Hiedler (Hitler) moved to Germany in 1913. Following his service in the German Army, he became a decorated soldier. He joined the precursor of the German Workers Party in 1919 and became leader of the NSDAP in 1921.

Hitler was imprisoned in 1921, accused of attempting to seize power. During this time, he wrote his autobiography and manifesto "Mein Kampf" ("My Struggle").

After his release in 1924, Hitler gained popular support attacking the Treaty of Versailles. Hitler frequently denounced international capitalism and Communism, as being part of a Jewish conspiracy.

By 1933, his party was the largest elected party in the German Reichstag, which led to his appointment as Chancellor on 30 January, 1933.

His first six years in power resulted in rapid economic recovery from the Great Depression.

Adolf was born on 20 April, 1889; the fourth of six children. In 1905, after passing a repeat of the final exam, Hitler left school. He worked as a casual laborer, and eventually as a painter, selling water colors of Vienna's sights.

Vienna's Academy of Fine Arts rejected him in1907, and again, in 1908, citing **unfitness for painting**. After the academy's second rejection, he ran out of money, and was forced to live in homeless shelters and men's hostels.

Hitler states in "Mein Kampf" that he first became an anti-Semite in Vienna.

In August 1934, Hitler appointed Reichsbank President, Hjalmar Schacht, Minister of Economics. Reconstruction was financed through Mefo Bills and printing money. Unemployment fell from six to one million in four years.

Hitler oversaw one of the largest infrastructural improvement campaigns the world had ever seen in the shortest period of time that involved the construction of dams, autobahns, railroads and many other civil and engineering works. His government sponsored architecture on an immense scale.

Hitler is blamed for the Second World War which is responsible for the deaths of millions of people; combatants and civilians.

"If the international Jewish financiers in and outside Europe should succeed in plunging the nations once more into a world war, then the result will not be the bolshevization of the earth, and thus, the victory of Jewry, but the annihilation of the Jewish race in Europe". [Adolf Hiedler addressing the German Reichstag; 30 January 1939]

Age of Oppression

The private wealth of the world is $241,000,000,000,000 trillion US Dollars. Almost half of the world wealth, 43% is owned by 1% of world population. The wealth of this richest 1% of world population amounts to $110 trillion US Dollars. [www.forbes.com]

Ten percent of world population now owns nine times what 90% of world population own.

Eighty-five people in the world own as much wealth as 3.5 billion people. [www.forbes.com]

Not even the economic crisis and recession of 2007 to date, has slowed these excesses or caused a rethink. In the US, the wealthiest one percent captured 95% of post-financial crisis growth since 2009, while the bottom 90% became poorer.

Seven (7) out of ten (10) people live in countries where economic inequality has increased in the last thirty years (with only China as exception).

According to the New York Times, the richest 1% in the US now own more wealth than the bottom 90%. Unbelievably, the bottom 90% own 73% of all debt.

Wealth includes the value of homes, automobiles, personal valuables, businesses, savings and investment.

The 2013 UNICEF data on well-being of children in 35 developed nations, placed the 'great' USA placed at 34 out of 35 countries – with Romania coming 35th.

That 90% of world population own just 10% of private world wealth is an insult. How can men call themselves civilized while allowing this to take place?

The system by which this extremely disproportionate share of wealth happened must be looked into.

Men are not born with wealth. We meet wealth on earth that we exploit. That which we make in business may well be said to be comprised of that which we gained from other men. Hence, we must exercise moderation or give back. Unrestrained capitalism has plunged the world into a situation where 90% of world population now does not own more than 10% of world wealth.

This system is promoted by the structures and policies of the governments of the world. It is atrocious that the majority of US population should own 73% of the country's debt, under the tiny fraction of wealth (10%) that they share.

The inconsistencies of state structures, like the banking (US Federal Reserve) and the tax systems which levy little tax on corporations and big businesses, further expose the connivance between capitalists and those we elect to government.

The scarcity of housing and the burdens we experience whilst trying to secure shelter (a basic necessity) leaves me astounded. Housing is a right of every individual. It is inconsistent that we cannot even afford a house on a large, spacious earth.

The earth's land is 149 million square kilometers in area. If we should divide this by 7 billion people, each individual would have a share of 3 square acres of arable land, after excluding the arid, desert or inhabitable regions of the earth. That would mean wealth for each individual in value as it pertains. Is this irrational? Then tell me whose land it is?

It is by cooperation with the aid of the state that we would now contribute this land – to the benefit and coexistence of all. Land should be rented off the individual and proceeds should be shared with the collective of government, which is responsible for the maintenance and management of the state.

The status quo proves that we are enslaved in a veiled system of domination, manipulation and privilege of the few. Its beneficiaries have gotten away with it by an elaborate and hardly detectable charade that has eluded us.

What has further engendered the massive inequality is the support capitalists receive from the government. Commercial banks for instance, enjoy inconceivable privileges and still manage to default, resulting in crises, like the 2007 recession. Commercial banks in the US can lend up to ten times their capital base and still charge heavy interest on top. No wonder there is so much debt. It appears that the commercial banks are getting free money and enjoying special privileges, while the masses wallow in hardship, extreme labor and debt. This is the same in most of the world, except China.

The Treasury Bond system is another one of the injustices suffered by the masses. Bonds are bought back by the government with huge interest on top.

The system is ridden with Interest. The cycle of repayment has driven many into bankruptcy. Governments have sunk underneath, with the ability to carry out traditional responsibilities becoming increasingly unsustainable. Government ability to carry out responsibilities has become nearly impossible without taking on debt and with it more and more interest. Citizens whilst slaving to meet their livelihood are faced with the burden of more tax in order for government not to suffer default.

How and why in the 21st century, does a minority continue to amass wealth while the majority and governments struggle under heavy debt and an increasing shortage of funds with increased dependence on capitalists to fund deficits. How or why should states struggle with less financial assets, while ten 'percenters' own 90% of world private wealth, is the injustice of our time which incomprehensively has provoked little or no revolt from the people.

It may be because those who have contrived to live whilst others perish or squalor in pittances labored for in circumstances similar to the days of Feudalism, employ a sophisticated strategy. Perhaps what is more explanatory is that those who occupy the offices of economic and political power are in fact not only alien to us, but lack the requisite nature to govern and co-exist in a world like ours. Furthermore, they seem to care little that we are financially destitute – living on high, above us, as we serve them like slaves.

Some have given up on what they term the "Rat Race", and make do, subsisting on the welfare pittances, in the parts where this is available.

The workplaces are a nightmare for those in employment, with various forms of harassment, servitude and intense physical labor. The governors and administrative overseers act as if the amount of work often involved is normal. They are constantly demanding more from employees. These pressures have made some suffer from psychological and psychiatric trauma. One thing we must note here is that the physiology of the Jinn differs from that of the Man.

Therefore, the Jinn may be more able to carry out the work which today demands much mental and physical effort.

All this behooves the question, who or what, are we working so much for? Are we working for ourselves or for external entities? Why are we killing ourselves to build pyramids? All the work on earth is for us. It mutually benefits us and helps maintain our world. Thus, we are working for ourselves. This excessive and in fact, 'killing' work – work system therefore does not serve us well. If one of the purposes of life is to achieve ease and happiness, then this work – work system contravenes it.

Do not let anyone deceive you about the earth's plentiful nature. It rains in abundance year after year. The earth is continuously made green and whole.

These capitalists satiate their greed and exploit the earth at the expense of your labor, giving you in-commensurate remuneration in exchange. The very resources exploited belong to you and the whole majority.

If people want to do business, they should accept its expenses, challenges and risks it comes with it. It is not for you or I to suffer in aid of their ambitions. The state, being ours, must always operate at the collective and equal benefit of its people.

In Africa, it is so bad that 550 million people do not own more than $60 billion US Dollars. The heavy handed politics of the states, coupled with IMF constrictions has denied many states the growth they seek. Electoral injustices and coup d'etat have made the necessary changes impossible.

The extent of poverty is shocking with inhabited conditions that do not meet a man's basic dignity. Here is where we see real despotism and the systematic crushing of the opposition by the armed apparatus of the state.

The increasing loss of freedoms of those in the western hemisphere is one of the most worrisome trends of all. The West has served as a beacon of hope for the rest of the world – for positive change, good freedoms and progress. The political and economic globalization in the last and this century means that one political system has taken over much of the world. The shift in the US from a state with incomparable rights and freedoms for its citizens, to a state that is increasingly amending its laws – leaving its citizens with less power, is a concerning trend.

The one-world status which the world is constantly assuming incorporates the extreme capitalism of the West. It could be assumed that any eventual one-world government may be operated under unfair, inequitable laws that could be draconian in the interest of its affluent classes. Capitalism remains largely unquestioned / unchallenged in the West (especially the US), which gives it totalitarian support.

It is safe to assume that 80% of the population in the western hemisphere holds approximately 65% of the debt, whilst owning 10% of its wealth. It is equally fitting to assume that 10% of world population will continue to capture 80-100% of future financial growth; similar to what was managed with the economic recession, now that the recession is over – with economic growth being recorded in most of the wealthy countries. This would mean a continuation of the cycle of the few rich becoming incomparably richer.

According to Plato, a state made up of different kinds of souls, will move from being a "democracy" to a "tyranny". Democracy degenerates into Tyranny from the conflict of rich and poor.

It is characterized by an undisciplined society, existing in chaos; where the tyrant rises as popular champion, leading to the formation of his army and the growth of oppression. [Plato's Republic]

It appears, I'm afraid that Plato was right and that Satan (incarnated) wants to rule the world. He rules in Valhalla (Jinn world) and intends to rule our world too.

We must now work to see that this does not happen before it is too late, and vote out these who cannot to date facilitate for us easier, prosperous lives.

Conspiracies & Terrorism

Humans (Gog & Magog or the Incarnates) enjoy one great advantage. They obviously have knowledge of themselves and can identify one another. They know who they are, and their collective mission. They have a hierarchy and a centralized system of one at the top.

With their identity concealed, they been able to operate from the shadows – from under this curtain; under various organizations, political bureau and agencies, to achieve their objectives.

The fact that we have failed to govern ourselves effectively and alleviate the hardship of masses, is in my opinion a phenomenon which before now had not received any convincing explanation. The previous chapter has already detailed some of the hardship and injustices now prevalent.

I put this to the man and woman. Would you if empowered subjugate and deprive your people of an easy and prosperous life? I believe that the man will not. The greed and selfishness of those in positions of economic and political power and governance, as well as their corruption is not shared by us. The tradition of further enriching the Bourgeoisie with aid of inexplicable policies and guarantees (like the bail out of banks) is not something you or I would uphold. The 90% who enjoy only 10% of world wealth do not own the money in the banks. Rather, they hold debt.

The sacrilegious dispensation of office toward the satisfaction of a few, betraying the oaths sworn and the constitutions of the land would be all too over-daring for you or I.

I am positive that women and men are bemused by those who make billions and give away little, if at all. The sheer hoarding and obsession with accumulating wealth is typical of the miserliness often associated with the leprechauns in stories.

The advantage which those who decide our economic and social fate have enjoyed is concealment. This has been their greatest instrument in conquering, succeeding leaders and achieving whatever of their objectives despite their fewer numbers. They are outnumbered six to one in this age.

Whilst researching, I stumbled upon a very insightful piece of literature which may help shed light on their matter.

"It comes from a very ancient democracy you see…"

"You mean it comes from a world of lizards?" "No" said Ford, who by this time was a little more rational and coherent than he had been, having, finally had the coffee forced down him, "nothing so simple. Nothing anything like so straight-forward. On its world, the people are people. The lizards are lizards. The people hate the lizards, and the lizards rule the people."

"Odd," said Arthur. I thought you said it was a democracy."

"I did", said Ford, "It is."

"So," said Arthur, hoping he wasn't sounding ridiculously obtuse, "why don't people get rid of the lizards?"

"It honestly doesn't occur to them," said Ford.

"They've all got the vote, so they all they pretty much assume that the government they've voted in, more or less approximates to the government they want."

"You mean they actually vote for the lizards?"

"Oh yes," said Ford with a shrug, "of course."

"But", said Arthur, going for the big one again, "Why?"

"Because if they didn't vote for a lizard," said Ford, "the wrong lizard might get in."

"Got any gin?"

"I'll look. Tell me about the lizards?"

Ford shrugged again.

"Some people say that the lizards are the best thing that ever happened to them," he said. "They're completely wrong of course, completely and utterly wrong, but someone's got to say it."

"But that's terrible" said Arthur.

"Listen, bud," said Ford, "if I had one Altairian dollar for every time I heard one bit of the universe look at another bit of the universe and say, 'That's terrible', I wouldn't be sitting here like a lemon looking for a gin." [Douglas Adams, So Long, and Thanks for All the Fish]

Gog & Magog are not Lizards or Reptilian. Rather, as noted earlier, it was Gog & Magog who brought reptiles like snakes, to our world. The snake may symbolize power, and men's aversion to it may have made it dear to them. Evil likes to corrupt fair and moderate nature.

I would like to see a man or woman who embraces the snake. Genesis mentions a serpent. Yet, I do not see how Eve would have tolerated or endured the company of a snake for one moment. If Eve could not stand the sight of a snake, and Satan, owing to this, did not appear to her as a snake, then you may be tempted to believe that he was in the form of a snake, but invisible to her. Otherwise, we are left with a description of Satan as the Snake of the World.

These people penetrated royal households. One example of this was Alexander, 'the great'. His mother would have had him illegitimately. The father's preference of another son and disgust for him is evidence of this. Men in most cases do not share similar character with Humans. Whereas, men are gentle, modest, shy and not so forward, humans tend to be different.

They can organize to win elections, and organize to control the agencies of the state. They introduce systems and structures which complement their smaller electorate, like the US, Two-Party system or the mainly tri-partite system of the United Kingdom. Political party control is paramount to winning elections. They field in candidates from among themselves and leave us with no other option. The only option, like in the quote above, is to avoid voting in the worst "lizard".

When they appear not to have numbers, their masses organize and come out, like they did in Livy's account.

Terrorism

The conduct of war in Islam is exemplary. You only fight those who fight you directly. You are not to harm women, children or the men who do not fight you. The act of killing men, women and children, who are not soldiers, has no place in Islam.

This practice was given legitimacy by scholars who issued "Fatwas" (rulings). These scholars do not have the legitimacy to do so. Those who may have the legitimacy to issue rulings, which do not contravene Islam, are the political leaders. Scholars have been given an exaggerated place in Islam that is akin to the place of scholars (priests) in Christianity. This is not something that was instituted by Muhammad, neither is it established in the Qur'an.

The office of cleric (sheikh, mufti etc) created by the Islamic leadership are concoctions whose legitimacy remains questioned – since there is no directive for this from Muhammad, neither is it in the Qur'an.

The audacious rulings by some sheikhs to give legitimacy or call for the free killing of people are both atrocious and lacking in authority. Propagation of Islam is the responsibility of every Muslim, the Mosque Imams and the state leadership. The establishment of exclusive groups of clerics is basically an innovation.

Islam is a way of life. As such, no one body or bodies could be established to maintain and regulate every aspect of it.

"And do not say about what your tongues assert of untruth; this is lawful, and this is unlawful, to invent falsehood about God. Certainly, those who invent falsehood about God will not succeed." [Qur'an 16: 116]

The problem we face is humans who have infiltrated our communities. It is they who carry out these barbaric acts that have never before been witnessed in the history of men.

The ambition of these terrorists is lunatic. There approach is not only uncompassionate, but severely lacking; and their philosophy self-defeating.

Apart from Palestine, where Muslims are oppressed, the non-Muslims in most parts of the world have propagated peace and sought to foster understanding with their counterparts. It behooves intelligent reasoning that the Muslim should also generate an understanding of the Islamic faith – especially since those in positions of influence had locked up parts of the earth's regions to Islam or propagated falsehoods about it. But we have failed considerably, to do this.

Islam and Muhammad were denigrated for centuries – even before the two worlds met (Christianity & Islam). Take what is mentioned about Muhammad in the 12th century by some. The man himself sent out letters to the Byzantine and Persian empires to inform them about his mission and objectives. These were generally disregarded. The only thing they may accuse him of is bringing and reinstating righteousness to the world.

Terrorism is an attempt by humans within and without Islam to pit the nations against Muslims, now that chance has presented itself like never before for men to know and in all likelihood embrace Islam. They seek to invert what is right, and the truth - presenting sin as alright and Muslims as forerunners to the Anti-Christ.

"Let there be no compulsion in religion. Truth is clear from falsehood." [Qur'an 2: 256]

"Certainly, those who believe, and the Jews, Christians and "Sabians", who believe in God and the Last Day, and do good works, have their reward with their Lord. No fear should they have, nor will they grieve." [Qur'an 2:62]

Tarnishing Islam

Islam, since Muhammad, has not suffered a greater blow than is now the case. Also, in Iraq, Syria, Nigeria and other parts of the world thousands have been killed in the name of Islam.

These abhorrent actions have left many unattracted to the purest Monotheism on earth. Think the identity; Muslim, and you first think terrorism.

The religion itself is so easy to preach. It suits perfectly the doubts we may have, and answers the questions that make many uninterested in other religions.

One does wonder what progress would have been made if not for this horrendous rendering of Islam. The strategy of the so-called Jihadists is weak. Even after conquering the whole world by force, would the conquered not resist or consequently free themselves from their subjugation.

Clearly, the only option is to convince by peaceful means the non-Muslim. Should he refuse to accept the precepts you wish for him to embrace, the errors of his lifestyle are there to make him adopt a better lifestyle, with time. If he should persist in wrong doing, then he will ultimately face his Lord, and He will punish him.

The Qur'an does make it clear that for the unbelievers is a short life of enjoyment and a painful future of torment. I find it hard therefore why you would not remain the patient believer and continue to restrain yourself from adopting extreme courses of action.

Is Hell not sufficient as a punishment? Why would you want to punish the unbeliever knowing that an eternal punishment awaits him in the Fire?

Muslims must rather concentrate on improving their lifestyle and as well improving their position through peaceful means whilst coexisting peacefully with non Muslims.

The verse above that names the Christians, Jews and Sabians is especially useful today in refuting these saboteurs. Judging from the last part which tells them not to fear, I feel confident in saying that this was not cancelled by God. Otherwise, it would not have an ending like that.

Portrayals in society and popular culture

"Power" Song by Kanye West

(Lyrics)

I'm livin in the 21st century doin something mean to it

Do it better than anybody you ever seen do it

Screams for the haters, got a nice ring to it

I guess every superhero need his theme music

{Chorus}

No one man should have all that power

The clock's ticking I just count the hours

Stop trippin I'm trippin off the power

(21st century Schizoid man)

The system broken, the school's closed, the prison's open

We ain't got nothing to lose

Motherf*cker we rolling

With some light-skinned girls and some Kelly Rowlands

In this white man's world we the ones chosen

So goodnight cruel world

I'll see you in the morning,

Huh? I see you in the morning

This is way too much I need a moment

{Chorus} ...

Among the things of note in Kanye West's song is the lyric: "No one man should have all that power." I believe that this lyric is referring to God here.

Also, 'the clock's ticking' is likely a reference to the end of the world. You must see the video if you haven't already seen it.

Schizoid man may give us another clue about the Incarnates. Schizoid personality is a personality disorder.

Schizoid man image online

"ET" Song by Kanye West feat. Katy Perry

I got a dirty mind

I got filthy ways

I'm tryna bathe my eyy, eyy, in your Milky Way

I'm a legend, I'm irreverent

I be reverend

I be so far (up), we don't give a (f*ck)

Welcome to the danger zone

Step into the fantasy

You are not invited to the other side of sanity

They calling me an alien

A big headed astronaut

Maybe its because your boy Yeezy get a*s a lot

[Katy Perry]

You're so hypnotizing

Could you be the devil

Could you be an angel

Your touch magnetizing

Feels like I am floating

Leaves my body glowing

They say be afraid

You're not like the others

Futuristic lover

Different DNA|

They don't understand you

You're from a whole other world

A different dimension

You open my eyes

And I'm ready to go

Lead me into the light

Kiss me, ki-ki-kiss me

Infect me with your loving

Fill me with your poison

Take me ta-ta-take me

Wanna be a victim

Ready for abduction

Boy you're an alien

Your touch so foreign

It's supernatural

Extraterrestrial

You're so supersonic

Wanna feel your powers

Stun me with your lasers

Your kiss is cosmic

Every move is magic

You're from a whole other world

A different dimension

You open my eyes

And I'm ready to go

Lead me into the light

Kiss me, ki-ki-kiss me

Infect me with your loving

Fill me with your poison

Take me, ta-ta-take me

Wanna be a victim

Ready for abduction

Boy you're an alien

Your touch so foreign

Its supernatural

Extraterrestrial

[Kanye West]

I know a bar out in Mars

Where they're driving spaceships instead of cars

Cop a Prada spacesuit about the stars

Getting stupid ass straight about the charge

Pockets on Shrek, rockets on deck

Tell me what's next, aliens having sex

I'mma disrobe you, than I'mma probe you

See I abducted you, so I tell ya what to do

[Katy Perry]

Kiss me, ki-ki-kiss me

Infect me with your loving

Fill me with your poison

Take me, ta-ta-take me

Wanna be a victim

Ready for abduction

Boy, you're an alien

Your touch so foreign

Its supernatural

Extraterrestrial

Extraterrestrial

Extraterrestrial

> Boy, you're an alien
>
> Your touch so foreign
>
> It's supernatural
>
> Extraterrestrial

I believe that the song is self-explanatory. The only thing I'd like to pick up on is the lyric which mentions Mars and spaceships. Jinn territory is not on Mars. Jinn territory exists over the earth on another dimension; as you may see in one of the lyrics. Yes, they likely possess spaceships and are more advanced in technology. If you are tempted to think that these are men corrupted by Satan, think again. These are not men.

Avatar (movie)

In the movie, "Avatar", the avatar is said to be "grown from human DNA mixed with the DNA of the Natives."

Among the key words to note in this movie is the Iwa (possibly Loa), which in one of the scenes is asked to transfer the spirit (life) from one body (Grace Augustine) into her avatar. Another is Pandora, the name given to the home of the natives. I suggest you watch this movie if you haven't already. You will make up the rest yourself.

As with every other public piece of literature or theatre, you will find only a partial representation of the Incarnates. The rest being jumbled information or plain fiction. The Avatar movie though is the first of its kind and perhaps the highest grossing movie of all time. The name alone tells you much already.

"Forever Young" Song by Jay-Z feat. Mr. Hudson

Let's dance in style,

Let's dance for a while,

Heaven can wait we're only watching the skies

Hoping for the best but expecting the worst

Are you gonna drop the bomb or not?

Let us die young or let us live forever,

We don't have the power but we never say never,

Sitting in a sandpit,

Life is a short trip,

The music's for the sad man,

{Chorus}

Forever young

I wanna be forever young

Do you really want to live forever?

Forever and ever

Forever young I wanna be

Forever young

Do you really want to live forever?

Forever, forever

Verse Two

… Fear not when, fear not why,

Fear not much while we're alive

Life is for living not living uptight,

See ya somewhere up in the sky,

Fear not die, I'll be alive for a million years, bye, bye …

With a little ambition just what we can become here,

And as the father passed his story down to his son's ears …

{Chorus}

Written in the Stars Song by Tinie Tempah feat. Eric Turner

{Chorus}

Oh written in the stars

A million miles away

A message to the main

Oh

Seasons come and go

But I will never change

And I'm on my way

Verse One

… I cried teardrops over the massive attack

I only make hits like I work with a racket and bat

… Adopted by the major I want my family back

The Representative

Adam was God's representative on the earth, and in this position he was excellent in conduct and head of all things on earth.

The idea of "the Representative" is one that should be taught to every child. It is exercising good conduct and leading by noble example, administering territory, animal life and in certain cases, the lives of other men, with integrity.

Man is a representative on earth, and in his administering of his neighboring man and the animals, he is to perform nobly and aim par excellence.

He is surrounded by a multitude of creatures; each with their own rights in a share of the earth. As representative, he must treat kindly the animals; some of which he keeps as pets, and do his best to ensure that they do not suffer. He should also follow good guidance and wise example. The most important quality of the representative is his acting justly upon the earth. He, without seeing, and in some cases having little knowledge of God, manages himself and the earth in an admirable or remarkable way. To some extent, he mirrors the greatness of his Lord, the Originator of all life.

He fulfills the essence of God in him which gave him life, in the disposition of his responsibilities, duties and in seeing to the welfare of all.

He slaughters with care and abstains from cruelty and wickedness of any form. He fulfills in proof the goodness of God and aims to achieve justice or equity in all matters.

Ultimately, he is thankful to God and seeks to know him well. Eventually, he is brought close to God by his effort, truth and goodness. His care for the world around him and the animals is a testament to all of his worthiness. He does not overburden or bring misery to any.

He may be loyal and impassioned for a loving God whose remembrance can only increase in him the need to be aware of his place and his God. Far from the heavens and free in will he is thus able to pass the test of earthly life put to him by God.

"He who created death and life, to test you – as of which of you is best in deed. And He is the exalted in might, the Forgiving. [Qur'an 67: 2]

His ultimate completion of the test is the confirmation of the will of God, conducting himself in a good way and executing good works. His primary nature is inclined to do good. This inclination to do good is the Man – the one who was made representative. **As with everything, God never fails.**

Hence, the man is successful, rightful of place and his good nature saves. Today's excesses has given credit to man's worthiness.

He managed the earth better when only he was on earth. The cruelty perpetrated on animals in experiments is evidence of this, apart from the millions now languishing in poverty.

Leadership

Leadership is key, in accomplishing an organized life, and for solving conflict which may arise amongst men. Without leadership, chaos could ensue. Delegation of responsibilities is achieved through leadership which coordinates the businesses and matters of men.

The leader is honored by the position other men give him. In this capacity he acts as father of the nation; whose interests he works to accomplish. It goes the saying: "The father cannot sleep while the children are hungry". He therefore, actively and proactively works to safeguard the interests of all.

The rain which God sends replenishes the earth and restores it to its fullness year after year. The leader, serving as overseer of the interests of all men must organize a system of extraction and cultivation of all resources with the direct or nominal help of every man. They must harness these resources to the use and benefit of all.

His position is not for the purpose of amassing wealth and aiding a class of people, or the stealthy glorification of his self and allied acolytes. That is the most base of leadership; leadership that glorifies in what is not his.

He is there because someone must represent the nation as one voice; keeping the ship of state stable. He is there to organize and establish a good and prosperous life that is filled with success.

Every man has a right to a part of the earth. Every man is a tenant of God who will eventually answer to Him.

The earth is collectively under the administration of men. The collective of men put what God has put in their trust (their estate) under the management or steerage of elected individuals. The end result must be ease of life and a stable stream of provision for every man or woman, adult or child.

No one individual is higher than another, except as it is with God – and only God knows this. His/her fact of being higher in God does not translate into a right to more.

The leader's position of management and appropriation of the estate of the collective should not serve as a gateway for personal aggrandizement or enrichment. Every man or woman may be equal to the task. They are all eligible to discharge these duties. For those who may want to suggest that leadership is for men alone, the Queen of Sheba was not only the leader of her people, she was given recognition by Suleiman (Solomon), who would not have associated with her if she were wrong to be a leader.

I fail to understand why men are poor when each man owns in trust a part of the earth.

Leadership serves as the cooperative for a prosperous and easy life, and is a means for combining skill and intellect – to exploit to our benefit the resources on earth. The collective of the estate serves to ensure efficiency and higher production. A leadership conscious of God is the best leadership, since it comprises the best of both worlds.

The current arrangement is while profoundly obscure, also confusing. Who really does land belong to? If it belongs to me, then why don't I have a piece of land to build shelter - one I can call my own. We have become worse than the animals under the tutelage of a few.

Lord of the Manor

Calls to abolish 'outdated' rights for lords of the Manor that serve no purpose in the 21st century – Independent newspaper; Thursday 16th January, 2014

"When 4,000 residents in Anglesley received official letters declaring that a lord of the Manor had served a unilateral notice against their homes to secure mineral rights beneath their feet, their response was unsurprisingly one of alarm…Stephen Hayes, who has spent 35,000 pounds Sterling on administering the title he holds covering 10,350 acres of Anglesley, is looking for a buyer, after receiving what he said was abuse."

A lord of the Manor was a free man who held land (a fief) from a lord whom he paid homage and swore fealty. A vassal could be a lord of the manor but was also directly subservient to a noble or the king.

The article (above) is just one instance of this gross, outlandish system. It is painful and almost impossible to conceive that one individual could possess 10.350 acres of land, to the detriment of others. Would men really be so insolently brazen, biased and unjust to one another – letting a thing like this pass centuries before - up to now?

At this time, when most of us find it difficult to embrace a belief in God, we face the end amidst the poverty or hardship that is now the world – with the climax of incomprehensible inequality.

Retaking our world

I hope by now, you will agree with me that there are amongst men, Incarnates, who form 15% of the world's population and now occupy powerful positions. This is kept concealed by groups, who using fabricated systems are adapt to quickly disparaging and reducing attempts to free the world from the clutches of those who continue in comfort while others perish in squalor.

This treatise is about Gog & Magog; a nation which according to Islam and Christianity will emerge, dominating and perpetrating much turmoil – close to the end of the world.

For millennia, their identity has remained under much cloud with many religious scholars struggling to identify and place them among the nations of men. The reason for this obscurity is in part due to the respite given by God to Iblis/Satan.

He, as already noted, instead of repenting challenged his Lord and vowed to subjugate men. His plan, as we now understand was to become independent of God. His plan was also to establish lordship for himself among his folk.

The facts presented in this treatise should have by now uncovered the, for long mysterious identity of Gog & Magog. This knowledge can now be used to retake our world and ameliorate the hardship in the most beautiful way and remove the "lizards" now in power, 'who some say is the best thing that ever happened to us'. I believe that by means of this new knowledge we can now establish a better life for us and the humans now co-existing here.

The vast majority of their own folk suffer too. That is the irony of selfishness. The Incarnates have either shown incapacity to govern like men in the world of men and an inability to carry out the responsibilities of man in his world, owing to some inadequacy in their intrinsic essence, or a failure to do so whilst harboring greed, selfishness or rooted hatred for men; or both. As such, we must retake those positions, by means of which we can bring about a better existence for all.

The election system of governance favors men. If you are fed up like me with the status quo, the good news is here. We can now vote out those lizards. We can now bring about ease and material comfort for ourselves and our children.

We should be sure of a minimum 80% majority in election outcomes. But how can we even talk about elections when we are not represented in political parties with Man leadership in the states we now live. The first move must be to establish political parties. Forget democrats and Republicans, we are going to start fresh political parties led by men. This will be the easiest of undertakings and the easiest, greatest revolution the world will ever know.

Identifying them has been made easy by the revelations regarding Gog & Magog. Their chief identity is the teeth. Again, the third tooth in the left/right upper row is pointed sharp, with a sharp tip. The picture below is a sample of a man's teeth.

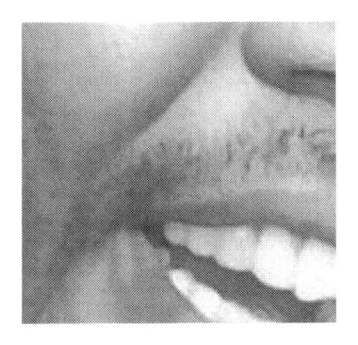

Theirs, Gog & Magog is a sharp canine tooth. Also, a keen observation of their right eye should reveal some oddness. With these two traits carefully observed, you should be able to identify one of them. With this identification, you would be able to garner membership and support for your party. You may have to travel from town/district to town/district in order to adequately strengthen your file, as their maybe a majority of Gog & Magog in your town or district. Rest assured, men have the numbers to rule and it is only with their support that you won't suffer betrayal at and pre-poll.

It is imperative for men to regain the political reins of office and correct this anomaly of economic failure, deprivation, debt and disillusionment. Men in the east and west must unite and free the world from the economic and political domination that has reduced us to socio-economic dilapidation, with many men now languishing in jails.

Man is mostly honest and upright. We don't get into political positions and loot the system. Once you start discovering men you will start seeing the difference in character, which brings with it ease and progress. Mena re not cruel to the suffering of people or the animals and cannot tolerate subjecting masses to a life of painful existence. In the same vein, you can now help your children or younger siblings toward social ease and comfort – enabling them counter the bullying and social exclusion they now suffer, while as well forging good friendships for their future. With your help they will not now be doomed by the 'Pandora woman' who you give your all to satisfy; getting little in return and children who despise you.

The banking system and its excesses, the Federal Reserve protecting a few, the bank of England and its monopoly, the stock exchanges and the inflation of prices by cartels that organize to pay pittances to farmers whilst making double triple or even ten times more and the Interest system which makes something out of nothing like in the case of the Federal Reserve/Commercial banks arrangement or the autocratic rule and overthrow of governments like the Libyan government, because it tried to make gold its trading currency does not have to continue.

The opportunity for purposeful unity that will overthrow the hoarders of wealth and the debilitating interest system, has for the first been presented to you.

Let us now organize as men to uproot this nonsensical system that has reduced us to hardship and cold labor.

I do not by means of this seek position for myself. I believe in self restraint and contentment and, a life eternal; great.

Men are suffering, and we can collectively act. There is so much wealth in the world; enough to sustain us with much ease. Since they cannot and haven't done better, let them give way for us to do what they haven't done.

"And We have already created Man, and know what his soul whispers to him; and we are closer to him than his jugular vein.

When the two receivers receive, seated on the right and on the left, he utters no word; except that with him is an observer prepared. And the intoxication of death will bring the truth; that is what you were trying to avoid.

And the horn will be blown. That is the day of (implementing) the threat. Every soul will come with it a driver and a witness.

(It will be said) You were certainly in unmindfulness of this and We have removed from you your cover, so your sight this day is sharp... On the day We will say to Hell: Have you been filled? And it will say: Are there some more? And Paradise will be brought near to the righteous, not far.

(It will be said) This is what you were promised – for every returner and keeper of His covenant. Who feared the most merciful in the unseen and came with a heart returning (in repentance).

Enter it in peace. This is the Day of Eternity! They will have whatever they wish therein, and with Us is more. [Qur'an 50]

Bibliography

- Larousse Desk Reference Encyclopedia; The Book People, Haydock, 1995
- Boelender, Douglas J, Eventful Archaeologies: New Appoaches to Social Transformation in the Archaeological Record
- The Greeks, Encyclopedia Britannica
- Flavius Philostratus, The Life of Appollonius of Tyana, Vol. 2
- Brewer. Cobham E, (1894) Dictionary of Phrase and Fable (PDF)
- Forsythe, Time in roman Religion
- Salzman, On Roman Time
- White. A E, New Encyclopedia of Freemasonry
- Sanolta. Takacs, vestal Virgins, Sibyls and Matrons: Women in Roman Religion
- Walsh. P G, Making a Drama out of Crisis: Livy on the Bacchanalia, Greece & Rome Vol. XLIII
- Horbury. William, (1992) Jewish Inscriptions of Greco-Roman Egypt
- King. Geoffrey Ray, Unveiled Mysteries
- King. Godfrey Ray, (1935) The Magic Presence
- Sharpin. Steven, (1996) The Scientific Revolution
- Brotton. J, (2006) Science and Philosophy: The Renaissance; A Very Short Introduction

- Lomas. R, (2002) The Invisible College
- Beck. Roger, (2007) The Religion of the Mithras Cult in the Roman Empire
- Clauss. M, The Roman Cult of Mithras
- Ulansey. David, (1991) Origins of the Mithraic Mysteries
- Hughes. Rebekkah, Happy Halloween
- Davis. Donald Leo (1983) The First Seven Ecumenical Councils
- M'Clintock. J & Strong. J, (1890) Cyclopedia of Biblical, theological and Ecclesiastical Literature
- Carroll. A, History of Christianity, Vol.2
- Hanson. R P C, (2007) The Search for the Christian Doctrine of God
- Rubinstein. Richard, When Jesus Became God: The Struggle to define Christianity during the Last Days of Rome
- CHURCH FATHERS: Life of Constantine, Book III [Eusebius]
- Maccoby. Hyam, (1987) The Mythmaker: Paul and the Invention of Christianity
- Brandon. S G F, The Fall of Jerusalem
- Pike. Albert, Morals and Dogma of the Ancient and Accepted Scottish Rite of Freemasonry XXX: Knight Kadosh

- Gyus, The End of the River: A Critical View of Linear Apocalyptic Thought …
- Magus Incognito, (1918) The Secret Doctrine of the Rosicrucians
- Arieh. Tobin Vincent, Oxford Guide: The Essential Guide to Egyptian Mythology
- Galpaz-Feller. Prina, (2006) Samson: The Hero and the Man
- West. James King, (1971) Introduction to the Old Testament
- King, (1986) The Cult and Calendar in Ancient Israel: Collected Studies
- Losch. Richard R, (2005) The Uttermost Part of the Earth: A Guide to Places in the Bible
- Walls. Jerry L, (2010) The Oxford Handbook of Eschatology
- Langner. William, (1968) Western Civilization
- Blavatsky. Helena P, (1888) The Secret Doctrine: The Synthesis of Science, religion and Philosophy, Vol.2
- Appollonius Rhodius, The Argonautica
- Smith. William & Wace. Henry, A Dictionary of Christian Biography, Literature, Sect and Doctrine
- www.mlahanas.de
- www.realtruth.org
- www.wikipedia.org

- www.sacred-texts.com
- www.icyousee.org
- www.metrolyrics.com
- www.azlyrics.com
- www.forbes.com

Printed in Poland
by Amazon Fulfillment
Poland Sp. z o.o., Wrocław